Square Peg in a Round Hole

Pastor Brad,

I hope you find this narrative "appealing," not the least regarding its Biblical perspective.

— Dr. Bruce
2/4/2009
MATTHEW 7

ALSO BY BRUCE H. JOFFE:

The Scapegoat

Personal PR

A Hint of Homosexuality?
'Gay' and Homoerotic Imagery in American Print Advertising

Square Peg in a Round Hole

Bruce H. Joffe

COPYRIGHT © 2008 BY BRUCE H. JOFFE.

LIBRARY OF CONGRESS CONTROL NUMBER:		2007905755
ISBN:	HARDCOVER	978-1-4257-6918-5
	SOFTCOVER	978-1-4257-6908-6

All rights reserved. No part of this book may be reproduced or transmitted in any form or by any means, electronic or mechanical, including photocopying, recording, or by any information storage and retrieval system, without permission in writing from the copyright owner.

This book was printed in the United States of America.

To order additional copies of this book, contact:
Xlibris Corporation
1-888-795-4274
www.Xlibris.com
Orders@Xlibris.com

*The people, places, and events described in this book are all real.
To protect their privacy, the names of most people mentioned here have been changed.
That being said, these pages are dedicated to Russ, my partner for life.*

1

FAMILY MATTERS

At the semicolon in time when the 1960s rebelled and retreated, me first, into the 1970s, my brother announced he was gay and cleared out his bank account to go live with his lover in California. Ken's devil-may-care attitude presaged that, if they wanted him in their life, my parents had better not *kvetch* but accede and accept him on his terms.

Which they didn't . . . and did.

I, however, was the firstborn but the last to relinquish control over my bedroom behavior.

Until I was ten, we lived on the lower level of a two-family home my grandparents owned in Forest Hills. It was—and still is—a desirable address in New York City's borough of Queens.

On weekends, I went treasure hunting with my grandfather to the empty lots and nearby junkyards where the sprawling Lefrak City and Rego Park housing developments still stand.

In 1959, my parents moved us to a brick row house near the intersection of Booth Memorial Avenue and 164th Street in Flushing.

We lived directly opposite a cemetery, next to Kissena Park, and just three blocks from the Long Island Expressway. Shunning our neighborhood's unenviable name, I still told people that we resided in the more upscale Forest Hills.

(Later, I could laugh about the location when *Northern Exposure*'s Dr. Joel Fleischman, played by Rob Morrow, told people in the remote Alaskan town of Cicely that he was a Jewish boy from Flushing.)

Surrounded by other middle-class Jews and Roman Catholics, we came from different places, but shared the common ground diasporas of upwardly mobile suburbanites.

Back then, Ken and I had twin beds bunked in one bedroom; Ellen—our only sister at the time—had the smallest; my parents, of course, commanded the master. We all shared the bathroom, which Mom had decorated with a garish foil wallpaper and reflective tiles over a salmon sink often splattered with mascara, Ipana toothpaste, and Wildroot hair cream.

* * *

I was fourteen when my mother became pregnant with her fourth child. Strange as it now seems, I never even realized that she was pregnant.

Neighborhood friends, especially the Catholics, didn't think another child was anything to become excited about.

I wondered, nonetheless, where they would put him . . . or her.

This decision was vitally important to me: I had withdrawn most of the savings from my *bar mitzvah* money to finish the basement and make it my own. Perched on a couch by our front window, I'd wait for my grandfather to arrive by bus early every Saturday. Together, we'd lay flooring, panel walls, install ceiling tiles, and build bookshelves.

Not six months after my room was finished and I had settled in, baby Linda arrived. My parents put her in Ellen's old room. Ellen got the room I had shared with my brother, and, now that the basement was finished, Ken was moved in with me.

It was awkward and uncomfortable. At that point in my adolescence, I needed my own sacred space, a private place where I could retreat to vent the raging hormones frequently expressed through ribald relief and nocturnal releases.

Really, it was quite embarrassing . . . even more embarrassing than when my parents got pregnant with yet another—a fifth!—child.

We were the only Jewish family I knew with so many children. I was seventeen, acquainted with the facts of life, about to begin college, and going steady with Mary Margaret Ritucci, an Ali McGraw look-alike six months younger than me who attended Saint Mary's Academy.

Despite her strict upbringing and parochial-school dictums, we engaged in heavy kissing, petting, and other forms of touchy-feely bravado. It was inopportune being reminded that our parents were sexually active. My mother's obvious condition, however, forced me to cope with that reality daily.

Actually, the pregnancy did have its brighter side.

I attended school from 7:30 am until noon, and Mom allowed me to take her car to school almost every day . . . which was a really big deal.

Among other things, my mother was very possessive. "I don't care whether I'm using it or not," she'd insist. "It's mine. And I want to know it's in the garage if and when I want it!"

Even on her deathbed, dying of kidney failure in a Florida nursing home, Mom retained ownership rights if not her deadpan humor.

"She's not going anywhere," joked Ellen, but Mom still refused to let my sister wear her mink coat to a show—in Miami!—or borrow her good china for an evening's entertaining.

Yes, Mom was a major influence in our lives.

Ken and I were secretly proud that people thought her attractive. But that was earlier on, when we still were infatuated with her.

Later, we struggled to deal with her bossiness, paranoia, and her martyrdom mantras. Mom always felt slighted—wronged by the world: her husband, her children, her parents, everyone.

Nanny and Grandpa had two children. Mom was five years older than her sister. My aunt was afflicted with Down's syndrome; the politically correct term now is mentally handicapped or "challenged."

Rather than institutionalize her, as several relatives suggested, my grandparents kept her at home, sent her to school—they didn't have special education classes then, but she made it through the fourth grade—and paid more attention to her than to her sister, our miserable mother.

Some siblings are compassionate, empathetic, and loving toward problematic brothers and sisters. Not Mom. She resented her sister and faulted her parents for their misplaced attention. And woe to any of us who took up their cause, trying to right the wrongs of the past.

Since he usually took the path of least resistance, Dad naturally shrugged and supported Mom.

Easygoing, gregarious, and personable by nature, our father was a big bear of a man who chain-smoked Parliament's recessed-tip cigarettes and allowed Mom to dictate life's terms and the family's agenda. He came across as the good guy, while she was seen as the querulous one. As might be expected, she resented him for that, too.

Dad, of course, had his own faults and shortcomings. When he started loan-sharking and peddling smut during my teenage years, Mom was torn between moral indignation and her newly acquired ability to buy diamonds, mink coats, and assorted costly bric-a-brac. She hated what Dad was doing but loved the luxuries his ill-begotten money bought her at Fortunoff's.

Now don't get the idea that I didn't—or don't—love my mother. Respect, however, is something different in my book.

As I told her during one of our many arguments: You can't control your love for parents; but respect, I maintained, was something they earned.

In her own way, Mom did love her children. She just couldn't show emotion or demonstrate her affection. It was easier for her to hug the dogs than to embrace us kids.

Whatever else, Mom was a fighter. That's what I told the rabbi when he asked my advice for her eulogy. Mom fought with her parents, with Dad, our neighbors, the school system, her illnesses, and more often than not, with her kids.

She just didn't understand what was going on with us.

Or, maybe she did.

* * *

I was six when I had my first crush. On Leslie Hofflinger. The neighborhood gang would sit on the Hofflingers' stoop, trading baseball cards (five came with a wad of gum in the Topps package for a nickel then), palling around and telling tales out of school. I always angled for the seat next to the good-looking teenager with wavy brown hair. I wanted—no, needed!—to drape my arm across his already ample shoulders.

Later, I enjoyed sitting in the stands of Yankee Stadium, cheering alongside my father . . . and played punchball and stickball with other boys on the streets of New York City.

I was a Boy Scout and, oh, how I loved the power that came from being designated a hall monitor and school crossing guard—craving the AAA's green, red, or blue metallic badge for its rank strength of sergeant, lieutenant, or captain.

Looking back at these memories, I was obviously too young to choose a sexual identity or gender predilection.

(Not that I want to get into a debate over whether we're products of our genes or our environment; but I believe that whoever we are and whatever we become are not simple matters with pat, rat-a-tat answers.)

Although many people will say we sit in the driver's seat, that we're able to spin the wheel of fortune and direct life's essential compass, I think the paths our lives take are ultimately mapped by some inexplicable logic.

I can't help but wonder, though, if anyone really knows how our steering mechanism operates . . .

. . . or whose hand it is that forecasts the fickle finger of fate.

2

The Damn Dilemma

The damn dilemma started with a series of adolescent encounters with Robert Petrovich when I was twelve and he was thirteen.

Robert lived behind us—our small plots shared a fence—and was the only child of Dominic, a Wonder Bread baker, and Theresa, who took the subway to Manhattan for work on temporary assignments as a typist.

On Wednesdays, New York City public schools closed early so we could go for religious instruction. Robert went to his church, and I'd go to *shul*. Later, those afternoons, we'd meet around the corner and sit on his stoop, where I'd test him on his lessons from the *Baltimore Catechism*.

The highlight of our week was always Wednesday, not just because of the school's early dismissal but because that's when the radio stations would announce their latest top twenties.

Robert would listen to WMCA and WABC, listing the former's song sequence in red ink and the latter's selections with a green pen. Meanwhile, I'd follow the play list on WINC, jotting down Murray the K's favorites in blue ink.

The next day, we'd compare notes, discuss the rankings, and predict what we expected to occur the following week.

Between Elvis and the Beatles, the radio broadcast bad news.

Dickens had put it best: It was the worst of times, the best of times. Although he was referring to another time and place, the same could be said for our Big Apple lives in the early 1960s.

Our own age of innocence, simple pleasures, and pastimes—of big, beautiful cars with lots of chrome and magnificent fins . . . of hand-tossed pizza for fifteen cents a slice . . . of Woolworth's, J. G. McCrory's, and other five-and-dimes—was threatened by looming cold war tensions growing more heated daily.

At school, we'd practice two forms of "take shelter" drills.

If there was enough warning before the Russian bombs dropped, we'd be able to line up, class by class, and march to the basement for maximum safety. As the bell pealed leisurely, we'd await the teacher's signal to leave, row by row, for the hallway, where a supervisor would direct us to the stairwell down to our salvation.

Should the bell clang more urgently, though, and we could hear the sirens outside wailing, there wouldn't be time to leave the classroom. On those occasions, we were to duck down under our desks immediately, place our hands over the backs of our heads (tucked between our knees), close our eyes, and look away from the windows, so we wouldn't be injured by the implosion of shattering glass.

We suffered these drills two, maybe three, times a week.

Outside the classroom, Robert Petrovich and I would listen to the grim radio reports and practice taking shelter in the crawl space under his basement. "When do you think the world will end?" was our perennial topic of discussion. We didn't speculate on how it would end—that we surely knew—but debated whether Soviet nuclear warheads would be dropped on us that evening, the next day, week, or month.

It was about this time that a dream of Camelot was born and began to weave its magic, spellbinding us as we followed the charismatic John F. Kennedy and his lovely wife, Jackie. Watching them wind their way through the campaign trail and into our living rooms, we'd sit mesmerized, snatching glimpses of their colorful luster from our black-and-white TV sets.

The candle had been passed to us, so Petrovich and I boarded the Q65 bus every weekend to trek downtown to Kennedy headquarters, a storefront located above the IND subway, below the IRT line, in the heart of Flushing.

We'd stuff envelopes, answer phones, and distribute literature door-to-door, feeling close to the action and far from our classroom.

Basking in the glow of our candidate's popularity, we buttoned his image onto our shirt pockets.

* * *

Somewhere en route to the Kennedy presidency and our newfound maturity, Robert and I began to fool around more seriously.

I was aware of an attraction to him, noticing (and responding to) the pituitary changes puberty had brought to his body. He was growing taller and broader. His strong, thickening wrists were masculine and notably appealing. And it was obvious that, soon, he could even grow a mustache.

I'd go over to his house almost every afternoon, where we'd turn the television on to *American Bandstand* and lie on the living room floor. Sooner or later, we began nudging and touching. Before we knew it, our clothing was off and we found ourselves turned on . . . messing around until we were exhausted and spent. We'd quickly get dressed and shun any more contact, making believe that what we'd done never really happened.

Our afternoon activities continued for about a year and led to later liaisons during the evening hours. Since his parents were home by then, we spent the time in his basement, doing homework and awkwardly groping each other under the table.

One night his father unexpectedly came downstairs and discovered us in *flagrante delicto*. By the look on his face, Dominic Petrovich knew exactly what was going on.

* * *

Eighth grade merged in a blur with ninth . . . nothing really special occurred until that fateful day in November when my class returned from its field trip to a Spanish restaurant in Manhattan.

We stepped off the bus and saw everyone milling around solemnly, in a profound state of shock. Word finally reached us via one of the teachers that President Kennedy had been shot in the head; gravely wounded, he was undergoing surgery in a Dallas hospital.

We couldn't believe what we had heard. Despite the world's troubles, awful things like that just didn't happen in the United States of America.

Time literally stopped, and our lives stood still, as school closed for a week so we could watch history's flickering images shot and transmitted by television: Jackie's bloodied clothing . . . the grassy knoll seen from that upper floor of the Dallas Book Depository . . . LBJ being sworn in on Air Force One . . . Lee Harvey Oswald's pursuit, capture, and gunning down by Jack Ruby in the police station basement . . . the caisson, riderless horse, and funeral procession . . . Caroline and little John-John, saluting his father, then kneeling beside their mother at Arlington Cemetery.

Something horrible happened that day in 1963 that forever changed our outlook, demeanor, sense of decency, and security . . . usurping literally everything we took for granted, believed in, and desperately had hoped to hold onto so dearly.

3

LIFE CHANGES

A fractious time of transition and fragmentation, high school was my own private toll-road through life's rites of passage.

As *Leave It to Beaver, Ozzie and Harriet,* and *Father Knows Best* gave way to *The Fugitive, Peyton Place,* and *My Favorite Martian,* I gave up the Wildroot and Vitalis for a blow dryer and preppier look.

I'd catch the Q65 bus two blocks from my house and take it to Jewel Avenue, where I'd transfer to the Q65A and get off at Main Street. From there, it was about a mile and a half walk to John Bowne High School.

Walking down Main Street, I'd have to be vigilant for the bullies who seized upon me and my friends as their own favorite underdogs.

I did like girls, especially attractive ones; there was no doubt, but I must admit that I didn't react to them the same way I did to the boys.

Though we weren't at all religious or hell-bent on avoiding anything sinful, I'd absorbed the notion that my feelings about other guys were somehow shameful and something to be hidden.

Except for the nasty jokes, gossip, and offhanded remarks, it wasn't an issue one talked about. Rather, you repressed your true colors and waded into the mainstream by focusing on girls.

A special young lady, I hoped, would help me overcome my latent feelings and replace them with other, more biologically acceptable ones.

So, I focused my attention on Mary Margaret Ritucci.

Going to movies, exploring French kissing, and getting to "first base"—she allowed me to unbutton her blouse and play with her nipples—or just hanging out, Mary Margaret and I went steady for almost three years. I escorted her to my high-school prom and she took me to hers, where the good sisters of Saint Mary's Academy diligently checked us over, measuring the distance between us and insisting we dance at a good arm's length.

* * *

That June, I took my girlfriend to John Bowne's senior prom, and she brought me to hers at Saint Mary's.

She remained home for the sororities and cotillions at City College of New York's nearby Queens College, while I left for the State University of New York at Stony Brook's would-be gallery of rogues, druggies, and dissenters.

We visited each other on alternate weekends, though our relationship lasted only a little while longer. It hurt, really hurt, when we ended it.

Pregnant six months later—though secretly wed, she swore by the blessed Virgin—Mary Margaret dropped out of school to make a home for the child and her campus Casanova.

4

LADIES' MAN

If television had been our high-school touchstone, music was to be our muse and hymn in college. As the sixties were consumed by the seventies, you could chart the changes we went through by our evolving taste in performers: the Temptations, Four Tops, and Otis Redding topped the list at first; they soon were overshadowed by more socially-enlightened singers like Bob Dylan, Joni Mitchell, Joan Baez, and Judy Collins. By the time I graduated in 1970, The Chambers Brothers, The Grateful Dead, Cream, and Janis Joplin had moved up to the vanguard of our spokesmen.

Eclipsing them all, of course, were the Beatles.

My Stony Brook colleagues and I forgot about our classes when the *Sgt. Pepper* album was released.

Like many of our turned-on contemporaries, we were convinced the Beatles had embedded a secret message on the album. With a little help from our friends—marijuana and hash—we spent countless hours cutting classes to decipher the words and subliminal graphics encoded on the jacket. Our conclusion? The Beatles were lonely and wanted to meet (and reward!) anyone sharp enough to unravel the mystery shrouded in their classic composition.

Over and over, again and again, we analyzed the words and interpreted the visual clues. Superimposed on the back cover lyrics, their stance and attire made it obvious that the lads from Liverpool deliberately had fashioned the letters F-U-C-K Y-O-U.

Picturing ourselves in a boat on a river with tangerine trees and marmalade skies, we followed the girl with kaleidoscope eyes down to a bridge by a fountain where rocking horse people ate marshmallow pies. Convinced that we were such a lovely audience they'd love to take us home, we climbed in the back with our heads in the clouds . . . till we were gone.

Eventually, we would become the Woodstock generation, but not before we had fanned the flames of social upheaval, military conflict, political turmoil, and sexual liberation.

It was indeed an age of division, dissension, and relentless rebellion.

Dormitories went co-ed, replacing open-door visiting hours and curfews with free love and cheaper sex. Bras were burned and black studies courses introduced, as African-American consciousness—and women's—began to be hoisted.

* * *

I hadn't planned to attend the State University of New York at Stony Brook; like Mary Margaret Ritucci, I just assumed I'd be going to Queens College. But when I received my letter of acceptance, I grasped the opportunity to make a new start in life . . . away from my family and my past; far from the elementary, junior high, senior high school, and college whose borders formed the 1964 World's Fair model "educational community" that entrapped our lives and threatened to imprison us with life sentences bereft of pardon or hope of parole.

When I arrived at Stony Brook for freshman orientation, the school was considered a quiet teacher's college in a picture postcard community nestled on Long Island's north shore. Overcoming the ubiquitous mud and silt enveloping the frenzied building everywhere on campus, we pressed on to our classes. Who would have thought our alma mater was well on the way to becoming a behemoth institution famed for its nuclear reactor and dissident mentality? We had no idea we'd gain such notoriety for being the first (and only) school to be busted twice in one year for drugs . . . the college of choice for free concerts performed by such groups as the Doors, Country Joe and the Fish, Mothers of Invention, and Jefferson Airplane.

Unaware back then of the difference between one's sexual "orientation," "identity," and "behavior," I clung to my hanger. Hoping that by denial, repression, and inversionary tactics this act would end, I attempted to dry-clean my dignity and lead a normal, acceptable life.

It wasn't always easy, nor did it necessarily work.

* * *

Rick was my roommate, competition, and nemesis, although we appeared to be best buddies.

With Don Johnson stubble and a racing stripe of chest hair that snaked its way under the elastic on his jockey shorts to a point just above his navel, girls found him drop-dead gorgeous . . . which they didn't hesitate to tell me.

Despite my jealousy, Rick and I were inseparable.

Many weekends and summer evenings were spent at my house in Flushing or hanging out in the Canarsie section of Brooklyn where Rick's family lived.

Two female friends, Gloria and Mary, also were roommates.

Mary Gravina was one of the most beautiful girls at school. With her honeysuckle charm, she could have been an Ivory girl on television . . . the girl-next-door who'd steal many a swain's heart. Gloria Berkeley wasn't quite so gorgeous, but her sparkling dark eyes, hourglass figure, and engaging laughter more than compensated for anything that might be lacking in the rest of her package.

Gloria was a French major, while I majored in Spanish, but we shared a couple of basic courses. Unfortunately, she was a sophomore when I was a freshman . . . something I neither admitted nor told her.

In our highly stratified society, the college caste system discouraged dating or friendships between older women and younger men.

Sooner than later, I became a sophomore, too.

* * *

Becoming more competent and competitive as a ladies' man, I began dating women whom other men desired. They coveted my "conquests," although, for me, these beauties were safe since they weren't what I really wanted. Somehow, I assumed that if the men I found attractive were attracted to women who found *me* attractive, then I'd be the winner. My prize? Acceptance and freedom from inner strife.

Case in point: Eva Rivera, a fiery Latin sexpot from Manhattan's Lower East Side, whom my friend Pete pointed out in our French class. We vied for her favors and—surprise!—I was the victor.

By our third date, Eva had spent the night beneath me in bed. Misinterpreting her moans for self-recriminations, I never penetrated beyond superficial humping, thumping, and bumping.

Nonetheless, when Rick caught us undressed and under the covers, the satisfaction I derived from his envy was equal to any orgasm I'd achieve.

I came close to falling in love, later, with Adora from a Spanish class. Adora reminded me of Natalie Wood's María in *West Side Story*.

We'd drive to some of the secluded beaches dotting the shoreline where we walked barefoot, hand in hand, through the sand as we shared our hopes, dreams, and aspirations. The mystical power in our passionate kisses and heartfelt embraces gave me courage to believe that, finally, I could have a fulfilling relationship with a woman.

If it weren't for Adora's roommates—five black women who earlier had accepted me but now, for their own reasons, rejected me for the color of my skin—I believed she could have saved me from my mixed-up disposition.

I spent a great deal of time with other women, too, although they were more often friends than romances.

Was it me and my fearful hang-ups . . . or did something unspoken restrict the direction and outcome of these *pas de deux?* Why was I content with mere friendship when, if pushed for greater involvement, I could probably score real touchdowns?

5

FORBIDDEN PASSIONS

John Richley resided in the adjoining suite. Though he'd sometimes join us as we sat around smoking and passing the peace pipe, John was basically a loner. Brooding, intense, and often morose, he liked listening to records of German marching bands.

He was kind of greasy, but muscular and hunky in a swarthy way.

Like most of us, John usually dressed in jeans; self-conscious and embarrassed by his hirsute body, however, his favorite shirt was a black cotton turtleneck, which he wore more often than not. While we fussed with our sideburns and groused about our difficulties in growing a full beard, John complained that he needed to shave twice daily.

One night, nearly everyone in our dorm had gone off to some concert that didn't interest me. Evidently, it didn't appeal to John, either. Strolling into our living room, where I was listening to music and attempting to read a textbook, John held out a joint of Acapulco Gold and asked if I wanted some.

Never one to turn down an offer to turn on, I said, "Sure." As we shed our inhibitions and my better judgment in the smoke's filtering haze, our conversation somehow turned to sex.

"Do you enjoy masturbating as much as getting laid?" he wanted to know.

Unwilling to own up to my lack of experience, I replied, "Sure," that I did think there was something uniquely exciting about satisfying one's own needs while giving free reign to private fantasies.

"Has anyone else ever masturbated you?" he asked.

"No," I abruptly answered, suspecting where this line of questioning might be leading.

"Do you think mutual masturbation would be erotic . . . maybe even sexier than doing yourself?"

Certain that this was the $64,000 question, I swallowed hard before responding. "I imagine it's different, but probably every bit as gratifying." I focused on the smoldering joint I was holding in a roach clip, so I wouldn't have to meet his eyes.

The silence weighed heavily as he waited several seconds before continuing. Finally, he came right out and asked, "Would you like to try it with me?"

Thus far, I had successfully repressed my physical attraction to men throughout my college experience. Avoiding any potential conflict of interest, I diligently focused on seeing—and being seen with—women. Sometimes, in the privacy of my room, when Rick wasn't around, I'd give in to temptation and allow my innermost fantasies to be coaxed along with my helping hand. But this was different. And it could be very, very dangerous. Throwing caution to the wind, I figured, "Why not?"

* * *

We agreed to meet a half hour later in the tub room on the dorm's second floor. Dressed in my briefs with a bathrobe tugged tightly around me, I arrived first. A few minutes later, John turned the doorknob. He, too, wore a bathrobe; but as he loosened his belt, I saw he had nothing on underneath.

Dropping his robe, he reached out and removed mine, kneeling to strip off my shorts. For a moment, we just looked at each other. John was big and already quite thick and hard, glistening hair sprouting everywhere—from the cracks between his toes to the crook in his neck.

Part of me cried out, "Yes, go ahead," while a deeper voice warned, "Don't . . . disaster." Self-consciously, I reached for him.

Guilt, disgust, and recrimination haunted me for days after that episode. I avoided John by every means possible.

About two weeks later, he stopped by to ask if I'd like to try it again. Rick had gone home for the weekend, so we could be more relaxed now . . . in my bed.

I obliged.

* * *

Over the next few months, John and I had sex several times.

The routine was always the same: He'd drop by to see if I wanted to "get together." I'd nod. He'd leave for about fifteen minutes—what was he doing during that time, I wondered?—and return in his bathrobe. We'd lock the door, take off our clothes, and get into bed.

One night when we were in bed together, one of my suitemates returned unexpectedly to find the door locked. He knocked for several minutes, but we didn't acknowledge him.

That was it! I'd allowed myself to explore these secret passions; but I forbade myself to continue this escapade any longer.

6

LIBIDO-IN-LIMBO

My first full-time job after college was teaching high school Spanish in Long Beach, a tired resort community on the tip of Long Island's southern shore. It was the last stop on the Long Island Railroad, and the train tracks literally divided the town in two. On the east side was uppity Lido Beach, with its fancy swim clubs and ritzy residences; to the west was grittier Atlantic Beach, littered with dilapidated pubs and pawnshops, cottages, and shanties. Smack in the middle squatted Long Beach proper, site of boardwalk arcades and a nursing home ghetto interspersed with low-income housing. Right off the main drag, Park Avenue, stood the Granada, a towering inner-city tenement transplanted to the suburbs.

I lived opposite the Granada in a two-room walk-up apartment above a print shop and real estate office on Riverside Drive. To call it a "hole in the wall" would do the flat justice; but it was the best I could afford, and whatever else, it was the first real place of my own. There were six units in all, including the super's double spread. My only windows faced the brick wall of an orthodox synagogue, literally six inches away.

It wasn't the Ritz, the super aptly reminded us when we complained about the water pressure, blown fuses, leaky faucets, or legions of cockroaches that scurried behind the antiquated refrigerators every time we turned on the lights.

I covered the apartment's linoleum floors with remnant carpets, painted the ceilings black with glittering stars, and pasted aluminum foil on the bathroom walls . . . way cool, back then! My mother traipsed out from Flushing with her Clorox and ammonia to disinfect the toilet and tub.

* * *

Persuaded that coitus would remedy my libido-in-limbo, I pursued sex as my own crusade in quest of a holy grail antidote to straighten myself out.

Sexual opportunity came knocking with my next-door neighbor, Adrienne Rhine.

You couldn't say that Adrienne was particularly pretty; striking is the term that suits her much better. Men were attracted to her, and she had lots of friends. Growing up in the Lido side of Long Beach, she knew almost everything about everyone in town.

Adrienne made an art and a science out of meeting new people—it didn't matter where or how she met them.

Some were commuters whose tolls she collected on the Atlantic Beach Bridge, where she worked as head bookkeeper; others were good Samaritans who stopped to help out when, parking on the side of the road, she lifted the hood of her classic Chevy in an attempt to panhandle.

Several times each week, Adrienne would drive downtown to Manhattan to mix and mingle at the city's clubs. She'd leave Long Beach at about eight in the evening and wouldn't return before dawn.

People were always coming or going from her apartment, and sometimes, she'd bang on the wall in the middle of the night for my help if she got into a predicament that threatened to turn messy.

I, whom she considered a nice but boring guy, soon became her pet project. Adrienne was determined to fix me and mold me into her idea of a *mensch*.

We began by enlarging my circle of friends. While I had been content spending time with one or two special people, Adrienne's idea of socializing was to visit as many people as possible in any given evening. Clocking ten minutes here and fifteen there, she'd run from this person's place to that one's in a whirlwind marathon. I was the tail, wagging her dog.

One evening after dinner, our regular specialty, franks and beans, Adrienne complained of an aching back and asked me to give her a massage. Laying on her stomach, she removed her blouse and undid her bra straps. For fifteen minutes, I rubbed her muscles. Amazingly, mine had become quite hard.

In the awkward silence that followed, Adrienne turned over and reached for my pants . . . pulling them down over my ankles and removing my shirt. I moved myself on top; but no matter how much I tried, I simply couldn't find the way in. Frustrated by my inability to perform to her satisfaction, Adrienne pulled up the covers.

"It's all right," she sighed. "You're still a virgin?"

It was more a statement than a question.

* * *

If my attention hadn't been focused on teaching school, I'm sure I would have lamented my regrettable lack of performance even more. But so caught up was I in my eight-period days that I almost didn't notice the lovely lass calmly knitting in my classroom. Her fingers stopped clicking their dainty minuet as she gently rubbed the pointed needle shafts. Tawny hair, parted down the middle, gleamed long and lush. Lips softly parted, her eyebrows arched slightly above light green eyes that bespoke something playful and mischievous.

Lynn Larsfield was a vixen, an absolute knockout. A senior in high school, she was eighteen years old to my twenty-one (plus a few months). She wasn't on the register, so why was she in my class? Obviously, it wasn't to learn Spanish.

She beguiled me . . . and I was enchanted.

After dinner at her mother's apartment one night, we kissed for an hour. Muzzling her breasts, I found myself quite excited. Lynn helped take off my clothes and asked me to stay for the night. The couch opened up into a full-size sleeper, we were comfortably enmeshed, and there wasn't any real reason for me to go home.

"What about your mother?" I asked.

"What about her?" Lynn countered.

"Won't she object?"

"Don't be silly. Why do you think she's in the bedroom with the door closed?"

I swallowed hard, but didn't need much coaxing. Despite our three-year difference in age, Lynn obviously had more experience. She pulled herself up and mounted me, guiding my manhood into buried treasure that felt so nice and wet and warm. Her cries and the rattling floorboards were bound to alert her mother, I feared, but Lynn said not to worry, that she and madame respected each other's privacy. We rocked and rolled ourselves into a sweat, until each was fully satiated.

Thrilled to have finally lost my virginity, I fell asleep hugging Lynn with a smile on my lips.

* * *

Lynn and I dated for the next year and a half. People marveled at her constancy and seeming commitment; I was the first guy she'd been involved with so long.

Determined to grab the brass ring and vouchsafe my newfound virility, I proposed marriage even though Lynn wasn't yet twenty years old . . . or the marrying kind.

She loved being the center of attention and believed there was nothing wrong with dancing or waltzing off with whomever she wanted. But I had a rule to which I steadfastly insisted: Wherever we went and whatever she did, she was to leave with the same person who brought her: me. Unfortunately, Lynn refused to abide by my principles or respect my wishes.

Dancing one night at a local club, she disappeared with another man.

Determined to maintain my sense of decency and assuage my wounded pride, I told her that was it; we were finished. I couldn't and wouldn't tolerate being cuckolded.

Three days later I learned from Ritchie Reitfellow that his girlfriend, Alice, had a friend who wanted to meet me.

I had met Ritchie through Adrienne, but we became really close during the time I dated Lynn, who lived near him and had dated his brother as well as a number of Ritchie's friends.

Ritchie was probably Long Beach's greatest male attraction. Perfectly proportioned at six feet and an inch, he usually wore denim overalls that showed off his bulging biceps, pectoral definition, and he-manly chest. Long, dark hair and a thick, well-groomed beard enhanced his big, blue eyes. He was the first man I knew confident enough in his masculinity to wear a pierced earring and have his hair permed. Despite his obvious machismo, I definitely detected something feline about him. Some extra-sensory perception drew us together.

Alice, Ritchie's girlfriend, complemented him well. Born in Brazil, she was a runway model of breathtaking beauty. Talent scouts and agents stopped her on the street, handing over their business cards and pleading with her to give them a call. Wealthy geezers and lechers naturally were attracted to her, too, begging Alice to name her price for spending a solitary evening with them.

Alice's best friend was Marie Demetrius, a shapely brunette with shoulder-length hair who attended nearby Adelphi University.

We dated for over a month, but I still was hung up on Lynn. So when Lynn called to say that she missed me and wanted to see me again, I broke up with Marie . . . but did the right thing. Taking her out to dinner, I told her how much I liked and respected her. Unfortunately, I confessed, I wasn't over Lynn and, therefore, couldn't continue seeing her. I really was sorry and hoped we still could be friends.

Smiling oh so sadly, Marie shook her head.

"Are you ever going to learn?" she asked me, then stood up and left.

7

OLD TRICKS

Lynn and I picked up where we had left off. Though I worried why she didn't get pregnant, the sex between us was phenomenal.

Or so I thought.

Not six weeks after we reunited, Lynn was up to her old tricks again. She'd break dates and make excuses for not being able to see me. Soon, an entire week had gone by without talking or being together.

One Friday night, I went out by myself. I was hanging out at a bar when Lynn walked in with a guy someone said was named Steve. She didn't even acknowledge my presence, nor did I say a single word. I just picked myself up from the bar stool and left with my injured pride.

When another week had passed without hearing from her, I mustered up my courage and called Marie, who graciously agreed to meet me for dinner. I apologized again for treating her so shabbily and told her what had happened with Lynn, swearing that this time it was really over.

Would she give me another chance?

Marie's radiant brown eyes dropped demurely as she placed her hand on top of mine.

"I don't think so," she stated. "Once a fool, shame on you . . . twice, shame on me."

*   *   *

Ritchie Reitfellow didn't have a phone in the house he shared with his mother and stepfather, so he came by wanting to know whether he could use mine. (Remember: these were the days well before cell phones.) Stretched out on the bed beside my night table phone, his denim overalls were unzipped almost down to his navel. His fly, too, flew at about half-mast—he wore nothing underneath—and I suspected he was blatantly hinting at something and making it known what he wanted. The ball was in my court: should I pass, dribble, or shoot?

Valor triumphed over discretion. I shed my inhibitions along with shirt and pants, modestly leaving on only my BVDs. They, too, came off soon, as did his. Lying there with him completely nude on my bed, I slowly took stock of the superlative shape he was in. But, relatively speaking, I was much better endowed.

Five minutes later, it was all over. We put our clothes back on without saying a word.

"I'll catch you later," he mumbled as he walked out the door, leaving me feeling quite guilty and more than a little perturbed.

"Later" turned out to be another week. Without mincing words, Ritchie went right to my bedroom. "I've been walking around all week with a raging hard-on that won't go away," he admitted. "Every time I think about last week, I want to do it again."

Quite willing to comply, I wasted no time climbing onto the bed and throwing my clothes off in reckless abandon. But he pushed me away when I reached out to hold him. "You just lie back," he commanded, positioning himself at the foot of the bed. Last time, we climaxed with hands on the masts . . . but now Ritchie's mouth took charge. While I never before had been willing to reciprocate, this time was different.

"I really enjoyed that," he said, grabbing his clothes and taking leave.

We maintained our friendship for many months after that, but never again gave in to temptation . . . nor did we discuss or even acknowledge what had happened between us. In the privacy of my home, we'd sometimes give each other a pat on the tush, a good-natured grab, or a quick little grope. But our agenda again was the pursuit of women.

Looking back through the lens of time and experience, I now wonder whom I thought I was kidding. Granted, lots of folks fool around with lust's many derivations. But at what point does it become less of a playground and more a prison for those of confined orientation?

I hated myself for the feelings I harbored and felt dirty, despoiled, rotten, and guilty. Wanting out of the dungeon that hampered heterosexual relations, I contemplated going for counseling but figured the problem was one of numbers: I had had more experience with men than women, and rationalized that all I needed was additional practice with females.

Marie was right: when was I going to learn?

8

Rainbow Colors

I licked my wounds and began to spend time again with my next-door neighbor, Adrienne. At least twice a week, Adrienne would go downtown to do the club scene. Though she'd invited me to accompany her, I usually declined. How could I traipse off to Manhattan at 10 pm, return after 4 am, and still get to work with vim and vigor by 7:30 in the morning?

Adrienne frequented clubs on the west side of the city, off Broadway between 52nd and 58th Streets. When I finally consented to accompany her, she dragged me from place to place, spending an hour here and a half-hour there, her usual routine. As we left the next-to-last disco after 2:30 in the morning, I noticed another club next door with a bunch of men milling about outside.

"What's that?" I asked, pointing to the building. "Are you blind?" she snorted. "It's a club for homos—men only. Want to go in?" I hurried along, grabbing her by the shoulder as we headed to my car.

Two nights later, I returned. By myself.

The club was called Hot Trots, and it looked like any other storefront disco, at least from the outside. A large plate-glass window was painted in an art deco motif. A beefy bouncer stood sentry at the front door, checking IDs and collecting cover charges. I approached the door, but couldn't—wouldn't—go in.

Backing off, I surveyed the street. Several guys were standing in front of the club enjoying a smoke and sharing some jokes. Next door, people were queued up, waiting to get into the club I had been to with Adrienne on my last trip to the city.

Turning away from Hot Trots, I walked over to the club next door and entered. Inside, I went up and down the steps, taking turns on each of its three levels. Nursing a watered-down screwdriver for over an hour, I wandered around, checking out the action and keeping to myself.

Sixty minutes or so later, I left. Once again, I ventured over to Hot Trots where a group of about ten men stood outside.

I leaned against the passenger side door of a car parked along the curb and waited. Nothing happened. By then it was about one in the morning, so I decided to stroll down the block. Toward the end of the street, I came upon a quiet building with a series of concrete steps leading to the front door. I sat down and waited some more, contemplating my agenda. What was I doing there? What did I expect—hope, want—to happen? What would I do, and how would I react, if something actually did? I needed a plan, a strategic course of action.

Before ten minutes had passed, another man joined me. In the shadows of the overhead streetlights, I couldn't really be sure what he looked like. Somewhat stocky, he was dark and wore a black leather jacket. If I remember correctly, he was a couple of inches shorter than me, and appeared to be attractive.

"How're ya doing?" he asked, holding out his hand for me to shake. "Paul." Obviously, he expected me to respond.

Affecting a Spanish accent, I said my name was Carlos.

I lied, saying that I was an exchange student from Spain and that this was my first visit to this part of town. He acted as if he believed me and shared that he worked in cargo administration at LaGuardia Airport, though he lived only a few blocks away in Manhattan.

"Did I want to go up to his place for a drink?" he asked.

Why not, I thought. I'd gone to the city looking for some sort of action. It had found me.

Paul lived about five blocks away, in a high-rise building where he rented a decent studio apartment—a good-sized living room, kitchen, and bath. I sat down on one of the two matching leather sofas that faced each other, as Paul put some music on the stereo set on a shelf above the fireplace mantle. Then he excused himself. Several minutes later he returned, wearing a terry-cloth bathrobe. He plopped himself down on the couch right next to me, draping his arm across my shoulder. We continued to talk as he unbuttoned my shirt and began to caress my chest. I sat immobile, a willing recipient of his handy attention.

He asked if I wanted to move to the other couch, which opened to a full-size bed.

As the bed was opened and he removed his robe, we nestled into an awkward embrace. Without thinking, I reflexively took him in my hand, wrapping it in a fist. It didn't take either of us long . . .

By then, it was after three in the morning. Paul began work at five. We showered, had a cup of coffee and a croissant, and he asked if I minded taking him to work at LaGuardia. We drove the twenty-five-minute ride in silence. He got out of the car and handed me his card. Call me, he said. Any time.

Returning to Long Beach, I was filled with mixed feelings and emotions. There was no question that I enjoyed the excitement of our brief encounter. But, even after taking a shower, I still felt dirty.

Another first in my life: a one-night man stand with a total stranger.

I fiddled with the radio dial to block out the conflicting thoughts tumbling around my mind and, ironically, heard the Rolling Stones singing: "I can't get no *satisfaction* . . ."

Coupled with a sense of satisfaction, remorse and guilt engulfed me all the way home.

* * *

Roseanne Feinstein had stopped in my father's downtown Manhattan retail store. Our family name was visible on the marquee, and she wanted to know if it was the same family whose son was (or had been) a Spanish teacher—specifically the student teacher she had had two years earlier when she attended summer school.

Yes, it was me.

Dad and Roseanne chatted for quite a while and she gave him her phone number. "Do yourself a favor," Dad urged me. "Call her. She's very sweet and really quite pretty. I think you'll be impressed."

Dad's concept of beauty and mine often differed. Roseanne Feinstein, as best as I could recall, was a chubby and outspoken girl whose principal passion in life had been playing the tuba. Unlike most of the students taking Spanish during that summer session, she hadn't failed the subject but was trying to get ahead.

I didn't need my father to play matchmaker and resented his constant questioning about whether I'd called her yet . . . and why not.

Nonetheless, I finally did call her and we made a date.

The Feinsteins were Orthodox Jews from the old country who lived in Queens, about 45 minutes from Long Beach. Tact wasn't their strong suit. In heavily accented voices, they let me know in no uncertain terms that their ways were different from mine. It didn't matter to them that I was Jewish; my kind of Judaism was worse, they believed, than being *goyim*. I didn't go to *shul* regularly . . . I didn't keep *kosher* . . . and with my long, dark hair, beard and sloppy dress, I looked to them like Jesus Christ or a slovenly hippie (the former was far worse, as far as they were concerned). Roseanne was a good girl, they stressed. More important, until I entered the picture, it was understood that she'd been betrothed to a man they approved of—a doctor from their country, Hungary, whose family the Feinsteins had known for years. Everything about the marriage was arranged and anticipated. Then I came along and upset their plans.

I guess Roseanne was reliving a schoolgirl crush at the same time she rebelled against her parents. It bothered me that her folks didn't like me but, ironically, I really liked her! Roseanne was smart, a sophomore in college; she had slimmed down quite a bit and dressed quite fashionably now. I responded favorably to her sassy sense of humor, and we really enjoyed each other's company.

As for sex, why worry . . . or even bother? Roseanne was a virgin.

Since her parents were so opposed to our dating, she had to make excuses and slip out to see me. That worked out okay for a while: I'd meet her on campus; we'd take in a movie or go out to eat.

When her folks realized that, despite their objections, Roseanne was still seeing me—and was now sneaking around behind their backs—they, of course, blamed me. They didn't want to lose their daughter, especially to someone like me.

If they didn't do something quickly, things would only get worse.

The Feinsteins called and asked me to come by and see them. Roseanne wasn't there when I arrived. Then they presented their position: While they had nothing against me personally, and were certain I'd make a wonderful husband for some woman, it couldn't be Roseanne. I wasn't from her world and she'd never be happy in mine.

Tearfully, they pleaded for me to break things off with their daughter. It might break her heart, but she'd soon get over it. Then she'd realize how right they'd been.

Saul Feinstein peeled ten $100 bills out of his wallet and handed them over to me. Was that enough, he asked, for me to leave and stay away from Roseanne?

I couldn't believe they were trying to bribe me. Worse, I later found out, Saul had called my parents to enlist their support. My father spoke to him, defending my "moral integrity." But it didn't matter or make any difference to the Feinsteins. They wanted me to leave their daughter alone, so she could pick up where she'd left off with the man they wanted her to marry.

"Maybe you should forget about her," Dad advised. "Her parents are obviously set in their ways, and there are plenty of other fish in the sea."

Yeah? How very observant of him!

9

TAKING REFUGE

Eating in the school lunch room surrounded by other teachers, I recounted my romantic dilemma and joked about the Feinsteins' efforts to thwart my relationship with their daughter.

Seated across from me was Barbara Graf, a student teacher. I really hadn't taken notice of her before. About five feet six, she had dark eyes and long black hair that almost completely hid her cherubic face. Barbara was married and hardly ever spoke, so I never had paid much attention to her.

My next period was free, and Barbara had finished her responsibilities for the day, so we lingered in the lunchroom and continued chatting. I learned that her husband, Mark, was a concert promoter whose clients included The Grateful Dead, Chicago, Seals and Crofts—big names in the recording business.

"You must have a pretty exciting life," I ventured.

"Not really," she responded, looking down at the table. "He's never home and, when he is, we don't get along. Mark likes to take charge and everything—what we do, where we go, who our friends are, even how the apartment is decorated—has to be his way. And I'm positive he cheats on me whenever he goes on the road."

Gathering my dirty dishes and utensils, I placed them on the tray and got up from the table. "Well, if you ever want to talk, give me a call," I said, giving her my number.

Barbara called that same night. And the next. And twice the day after that. She said she was curious about what was going on with Roseanne. But I learned more about her life than she did about mine during our conversations. Barbara said she married Mark, in part, because of her controlling father, who was always trying to adjust her life, as well as to take some of the limelight away from her Barbie doll cousin, Bonnie, who had just gotten married herself.

Barbara and I began to spend more time together. She'd stop by my place after school, call every evening, and come to the beach with me on the warmer weekends. Once, several of her students saw us lying on a blanket together, our feet buried in the sand.

"Hi, *Mr.* Graf," they scoffed, and we knew that word would soon get around school that we had been seen together.

We shared secret concerns and private thoughts in the course of our friendship, so I came to know quite a bit about Barbara. I learned how uptight she was about her weight. Barbara didn't eat. An apple—one piece of fruit—was all she allowed herself every day. Nevertheless, for some reason she couldn't lose any pounds.

Her weight and eating habits quickly became a point of contention between us. Barbara asked if I thought she was too heavy, and I insisted "no," but she could lose a few pounds if it mattered that much to her. Barbara insisted I never had noticed or paid attention to her because of her weight, while I maintained that that had nothing to do with it.

For one thing, I was involved with someone else; for another, she was married, and I didn't make a habit of intruding on another man's territory. Then, too, there was that other reason.

* * *

My involvement with Roseanne soon resolved itself as we got together one last time. I told her I couldn't deal with her parents' hostility and was too old to continue sneaking around like some sort of schoolboy.

Barbara's marriage resolved itself, too.

She called me one night from the phone in her bathroom, where she had taken refuge from the birthday party Mark had arranged for her with his friends. He was stoned out of his mind, music was blasting, the apartment was in shambles. Barbara was leaving him. Would I come to get her? Could she stay with me?

Barbara was waiting outside when I drove up, a small suitcase in her left hand and two plastic kitchen bags with her grandmother's collection of Hummel figurines in her right. She'd written Mark a note telling him their marriage was over, and left it on his bedroom nightstand. If it was all right with me, we'd come back tomorrow after Mark had left to collect the rest of her things.

That night, we slept together for the first time.

We drove back to her place the next afternoon. I parked across the street from the three-story apartment. Barbara said she'd go in alone, see if Mark was home, and face the music if he was. He wasn't, but she asked me to come in to hear the music Mark had left for her to hear.

Playing continuously on the loop-to-loop tape deck was Elvis Presley, crooning, "You don't know what you have until you lose it."

As we left with Barbara's remaining possessions, she replaced Mark's tape with a musical message of her own: Carole King, singing "It's too late . . ."

10

LOOSE ENDS

Barbara moved in with me and we began to scale the major and minor chords of living together. Our two major disputes concerned her eating habits—Barbara still refused to ingest anything more than an apple or the dry skin of a baked potato—and drugs. While she refused to consume any food, she would swallow several Quaaludes each day.

About a month after she moved in, Barbara's parents came up for a visit. Since they despised Mark and were crushed when Barbara married him, they were thrilled that she had left him. Their support and encouragement, however, didn't extend to Barbara's decision to move in with me. Accusing their daughter of being a "bed hopper," they urged her to come back to Maryland where they could take care of her and she could give her body a break from all the "medicines" she'd been taking.

Barbara's mother, Belle, was a tiny blonde woman with a large heart and expressive blue eyes full of feeling. Her *oigen,* as Jewish people called them, referred to fluttering eyelids that, much like a metronome, kept beat with her fugue of cares and concerns.

Phil, on the other hand, was a loaded shotgun ready to be fired. Just about five feet, five inches tall, with a full head of slicked back, shiny black hair, he reminded me a lot of Robert Blake as *Baretta*. I nicknamed him Napoleon, a tribute to his stern, disciplinarian attitude and dictatorial disposition.

As Phil took Barbara aside to give her advice and see if she needed anything, Belle grabbed my hand. "I can see that you really do care about her," she said, fixing her fluttering eyes intently on mine. "Promise me you'll take care of her."

Before they left, we reached a compromise with Barbara's parents: They resolved to stop pleading with Barbara about moving home if we, in turn, agreed to spend our spring recess with them in Maryland.

* * *

We packed our suitcases, jumped in the car, and headed south, crossing the Verazzano Bridge and going onto I-95 along the New Jersey Turnpike, across the Memorial Bridge into Delaware and, a few miles later, Maryland. We exited at the Capital Beltway, which we followed to Silver Spring where Barbara's folks lived in a large split level house in Wheaton, a middle-class Jewish neighborhood off University Drive.

We were living together in Long Beach, but that was another world and a lifestyle away. Under Phil's roof, the rules were quite different: Barbara would sleep in her own bedroom with its pretty white furniture and delicate draperies; my barracks were brother Bob's spartanly furnished room with a captain's bed, armoire, and gun cabinet.

The highlight of our trip was a brief excursion to Columbia, Maryland, a model city being built midpoint between Baltimore and Washington, D.C. Pristine neighborhoods boasted beautiful home sites, apartments, and condominiums. Community centers, schools, pools, bike and jogging trails were strategically placed throughout. In addition to a dozen or so local shopping centers conveniently arranged within walking distance of each "village," a magnificent mall was centrally located in Columbia. Since the city was built

SQUARE PEG IN A ROUND HOLE

from scratch, it had no natives. Everyone who lived in Columbia chose to move and settle there. And, why not? Not only was each aspect of the community planned to perfection, but everything was new and pretty inexpensive. I was paying over $150 a month for an old, decrepit hole in the wall when I could rent a spacious, two-bedroom apartment in Columbia with solid wood floors, a dishwasher, washing machine, and dryer for only $130—including utilities. This was the early 1970s, when gasoline cost 32 cents per gallon!

Driving back to Barbara's folks, we compared New York's dingy grocery stores—Bohack, Associated, Waldbaums, and Key Food—to the more modern, well-lit Giant. We contrasted Alexander's and Klein's department stores with the much nicer Hecht's and Woodie's. We calculated the cost of living against the quality of life in each place. And we discussed the potential problems of living so close to Barbara's parents.

Never really a risk-taker, I worried about giving up my job to move to a new city, 250 miles away. Yet, financially unencumbered, we were young, and there were two of us capable of contributing to our living expenses. Before getting out of the car, we had made up our minds: Columbia, here we come!

With some trepidation, I handed in my resignation two weeks later. We tied up loose ends; sold most of my bachelor furniture; rented a U-Haul to transport our clothing, keepsakes, and remaining possessions; and said our goodbyes. Heading off to Maryland with a trailer hitched to the rear of my car, we bade farewell to Long Beach.

So much had happened there half a lifetime ago, it was hard not to look back. I still keep in touch with some people and visit from time to time, hearing updates on their loves and lives.

Lynn married a pilot and enjoys an open marriage, I'm told. Adrienne's become the biggest (and best) black jack dealer in Las Vegas. Roseanne Feinstein married her doctor, has two beautiful children, and presides over the women's auxiliary and PTA in a San Diego suburb.

BRUCE H. JOFFE

Poor Ritchie Reitfellow turned gray quite early and married someone other than Alice. They divorced not six months later. He joined the army for the educational opportunities it offered but was sent to Vietnam where a land mine blew off his leg. Ritchie lives among the homeless now, I hear. Although we live over six hours apart, I could swear that I sometimes see him on the highways—thumb raised—trying to hitch a ride.

11

MINOR IRRITATIONS

We arrived in Columbia with relatively few furnishings but a lot of old baggage. My folks were moving to Florida and would be shipping us their bedroom set. There must be some psychological significance to my misgivings about sleeping on my parents' mattress, but our budget was limited, and it was one less expenditure to strain our finite bank account.

Barbara's annulment from Mark was finalized before we left Long Beach. After she took the witness stand, swearing that he had deceived her and lied about wanting to have children, I was called to testify. My role in the proceedings was to recount how, when I picked him up from the bathroom floor in a drug-induced stupor and laid him on his bed during our final visit to their apartment, Mark had told me he hated children.

Deception was Barbara's pet peeve and the relationship wrecker she most dreaded. "Whatever happens between us, promise me you'll be truthful," she pleaded with me. "If you no longer love me or find someone else, just be honest. I'd much rather find the truth out from you than hear it from someone else, like happened with Mark."

No problem, I agreed, and solemnly swore to be honest with her.

* * *

The second week of August, Barbara got a job offer from a nearby facility for emotionally troubled youngsters. Though her degree was in English and her teaching credentials in secondary education, Barbara didn't want to work with the "normal" kids she found spoiled and unchallenging. Handicapped children were more demanding in some ways, but Barbara preferred dealing with their problems.

A week later, the teacher placement service I had registered with called to tell me they had a possible job lead. Was it true I had taught before in an innovative setting based on individualized instruction? How far was I willing to travel? Would I consider working in a parochial school? The position they were recruiting for was chairman of the foreign language department at a progressive all-boys Catholic high school in Alexandria, Virginia—over 50 miles away.

I was impressed with both Bishop Ireton High School and the Oblates of St. Francis de Sales, the priests charged with running it. The men were mostly young and quite liberal—at least in terms of their educational philosophy. Unlike the conservative Christian institutions I previously had been exposed to, Bishop Ireton's radical approach to instruction included tearing down walls so students could learn in a more open environment. Structured classroom instruction would be replaced with self-paced and self-directed curriculum materials created by teachers. Even the role of teachers was being revamped, substituting paraprofessional support staff and multi-media centers to handle some instructional tasks. Experiential learning opportunities outside the school were stressed, taking advantage of the treasure trove of resources in the national capital area.

If I accepted the position, I wasn't expected to attend mass or participate in other religious activities. Nor would I be a total stranger in a strange land. Another Jewish person, the school librarian, already worked at Bishop Ireton.

For a Catholic school, the salary wasn't bad. Faculty members were pleasant, the job seemed exciting, and it came with full benefits. The only problem was transportation. With jobs in different locations, Barbara and I needed another car . . . a reliable one, since I'd be driving over 500 miles a week now.

Barbara and I looked at lots of new cars. I liked a bright red Datsun; she favored a white Toyota. We compromised on a gray Honda. Before signing the papers and taking delivery, however, Barbara suggested we ask her father for his opinion. Phil owned an automobile supply store, and if we ever needed any parts or service, he'd take care of us.

Phil recommended we stick with a solid, American vehicle. Swallowing my pride, I ended up buying a bland, mustard-colored 1973 Dodge Swinger. The car came with a vinyl roof, power steering and brakes, and an AM/FM radio. It wasn't what I envisioned myself driving, but qualified as reliable transportation. In the five years we owned it, the body rusted and corroded, but nothing mechanical ever went wrong.

* * *

The Oblates had compassion for my long daily trek and invited me to join them for breakfast each morning in the rectory adjoining the school building. Over orange juice, coffee, and croissants, we discussed topics ranging from philosophy and ethics to religion. I knew little about Judaism, let alone Christianity, so I agreed to the priests' suggestion that I read the New Testament. Reading the book couldn't hurt, I reasoned, and it was the least I could do to show my respect and professional gratitude.

As I read through the gospels of Matthew, Mark, Luke, and John into the Acts of the Apostles and their letters, I was taken with the compelling story and how consistent it seemed to be with what I remembered of the Old Testament Scriptures, which my people believed.

Surprisingly, I had no trouble swallowing such complex doctrine as the virgin birth, Trinitarianism, or resurrection from the dead—the principal stumbling blocks separating Judaism from Christianity.

In spite of my open mind and willingness to acknowledge the possible veracity of their mother church's cardinal principles, I couldn't comply with the good fathers' invitation to become a Catholic.

* * *

One of the perks of teaching foreign language in an affluent school is that you're asked to accompany students abroad during their holidays and vacations. Several parents had asked me to consider chaperoning their sons on a trip to Spain over Easter recess. All of my expenses would be paid and, if more than twelve were in our group, Barbara's trip would also be covered.

There was only one fly in the ointment: For the school to sanction (and the priests to bless) our excursion, Barbara and I would have to be married. It wouldn't be proper—and parents would probably object—to have an unmarried couple sharing accommodations under the know-it-all scrutiny of a bunch of Catholic boys. What kind of example would that set, especially during the Holy Week celebration in Spain over Easter?

Marriage wasn't out of the question for us; it was more a matter of *when*. Barbara still bore the scars from her first marriage and was hesitant to make a commitment. But we had spent over ten months together in a healthy, soulful communion, and she knew that I was quite different from Mark. For my part, a pledge of eternal commitment held the prospect of helping me lock up the temptation to act on any feelings I still harbored for other men.

In all our time together, I hadn't wandered and had been faithful.

We decided to take the plunge, and set a March wedding date. Neither of us wanted a large, elaborate ceremony; we preferred our nuptials to take place at home, in the familiar setting of Belle and Phil's house. Neighbors, friends, and family did most of the cooking and decorating. My folks drove in from New York. The night before the service, we gathered for a formal dinner at an elegant restaurant. After exchanging vows officiated by a popular reform rabbi we'd met in Columbia, our late-afternoon reception followed at Barbara's childhood home.

Although our ties were legal now, matrimony didn't really change our relationship (for better or for worse), except that Barbara now wore a lovely cocktail wedding band my mother had discovered at Bloomingdale's; a simple gold band Barbara picked out encircled the ring finger of my left hand. For years, that ring would be my security blanket, as I defensively displayed it any time I sensed someone—a man—looking me over and checking me out, gauging the possibility of my interest and availability.

Two weeks after the wedding, we left for thirteen days in Spain. Our honeymoon included fifteen parochial school boys from Bishop Ireton.

* * *

We returned home to an unexpected surprise: During our absence, my folks had conferred with Barbara's and agreed to give us the money for a down payment on our own home. Barbara had been offered a full-time position beginning in the fall, teaching special education in Prince William County. We decided to look for a house in Manassas, where the cost of living was still quite affordable.

Before Lorena Bobbit cut off her husband's penis and put Manassas on the map, the Washington suburb was considered the outer limits—about 45 minutes from my job at Bishop Ireton and our Alexandria apartment. The drive from the Beltway and out I-66 seemed to take forever. Our destination had only one main drag, which was filled with fast-food restaurants, shopping plazas, and a nondescript mall; the media mockingly referred to Sudley Road as the "Fifth Avenue of Manassas."

Nevertheless, we fell in love with an adorable, two-level townhouse in a development called Country Scene. Contemporary in design with a step-down living room, huge country kitchen, three bedrooms, one full bath and powder room, our new home cost $36,990. We closed on the house at the beginning of June and moved in a week later.

I enjoyed playing Joe Homeowner, painting and hanging shelves during our two months of summer vacation. Barbara used her time off from school to catch up on her "stories," the daytime soap operas she had watched when she visited her grandmother after elementary and junior high school.

I found myself sneaking into the bedroom to get a look at the faces of the televised people uttering such melodramatic statements. Barbara filled me in on their histories. Before long, I found myself sitting on the bed watching. Quickly getting caught up in their problems and entanglements, I soon realized that I was hooked.

12

FANS, FEARS, AND FANTASIES

Soap opera fans can indulge their fears and fantasies as they cannot in real life. These serialized stories allow viewers to become part of a world far richer in material for jealousy, envy, relief, and disdain than even the most lively gossip could crave. Nowhere else in society does anyone have an opportunity to see how other people behave in such intimate, compromising, and volatile situations.

About 35 million people spend time every day with this convoluted community of characters who've endured more horrors than concentration camp survivors. Each show seemed to have its own characteristics.

Naturally, I had my favorites. I liked *Edge of Night* best, since it had less contrived romance and more crime and mystery, making it more of a "who-done-it?" serial. I also enjoyed *The Young and the Restless* because it was the quickest moving, and the people were all so incredibly beautiful. I had become loyal to *Another World*, Barbara's favorite, since we'd watched it the longest together, and to *Somerset*, an *Another World* spin-off.

* * *

BRUCE H. JOFFE

Before school ended for the summer, the principal of Bishop Ireton asked me to take on the responsibility of putting together an alternative adult education program. Rather than the run-of-the-mill conversational Spanish, dog obedience training, and small business accounting courses that most local schools offered, Bishop Ireton wanted to do something different.

Among the classes I proposed, one revolved around daytime dramas: their characters, stories, audience profile, and the role they might play in exposing social issues, as well as how soaps actually affect the lives of their viewers. I called my course Soap Opera Sociology and put out a press release to announce it. The media had a field day.

The Washington Post insisted I was trying to make "silk out of a sow's ear." *NewsCenter 4* sent a reporter to cover our first session. I was asked to appear on *Good Morning, Washington; Take It From Here;* and *Panorama* (with Phyllis Diller). In addition, invitations came from two community colleges and the University of Maryland for me to teach my soap opera class on their campuses. I accepted the Maryland offer.

As a result of all this publicity, I became somewhat of a celebrity. Dubbed the "Soap Opera Sociologist," I found I could market my exposure into a profitable enterprise. A lecture agency lined up speaking engagements for me at colleges and civic groups around the country. Talking about the soaps led to writing a weekly syndicated newspaper column. And that led to an opportunity to write for the soaps themselves.

My professorial podium at the University of Maryland made it easy for me to interact with the three networks and request guest speakers. ABC, CBS, and NBC were delighted to comply since every time they dispatched actors, actresses, producers, directors, and writers to Washington, they generated publicity by arranging for these spokespeople to appear on talk shows of the networks' local affiliate stations. I was often invited to appear with them and discuss the shows from a Soap Opera Sociologist perspective.

Edge of Night's head writer was impressed with my grasp of soap operas and wanted to know if I'd ever considered writing for the shows. Even though I hadn't, he asked me to submit a sample script and then offered me a job as writer for his show.

Between my new responsibilities—I'd work at home and travel to confer with the production staff once or twice each month—and my lecture commitments, not to mention the weekly newspaper column I wrote, there weren't enough hours in the day or days in the week to do everything. Something had to give. I was earning twice as much from my soap opera activities than from teaching, so, financially, there was little to think about.

Besides, I enjoyed the jet-set life which had opened up to me, hobnobbing with celebrities I knew on a first-name basis now.

Barbara, too, loved the fantasy world we moved in as she became friendly with the actors and actresses she'd only known on the tube. A brief walk-on role I arranged for her on *Edge of Night* gave her celebrity status among her school's teachers and students.

In March, I handed in my resignation to Bishop Ireton, using the sick time and personal leave days I'd accumulated to fulfill my outside obligations and commitments.

Starting in June, my full-time efforts would be devoted to soap operas.

13

RAGING REVELRY

Soap opera writers have lucrative yet challenging jobs. Before a show premiers, producers and writers come up with a "bible" that delineates all characters within the story's context. Not only are the storyline's twists and turns generally projected for years into the future, but a multi-generational background known as the "back story" is created for each character. Working with the sponsor—generally Procter & Gamble—the head writer then plots a year's worth of more specific storylines which, in turn, are translated into thirteen week arcs. Actors sign 13-week contracts, guaranteeing them specific amounts of air time. It's the job of a show's writers to come up with scripts that both advance the plot and give performers the exposure to which their contracts entitle them for those thirteen weeks. That's why there's so much repetition and why the daytime stories tend to move so slowly.

Generally, writers are assigned to work on one week of episodes at a time. Some shows give each writer a specific day's script, while others team up their writers on one or more. After writing the scripts, we'd all meet to share what we'd created and review it for accuracy and faithfulness. It was fun, if tedious, work, and I often wondered how many times we could have our characters emote, "It's all right, dear. Do you want to talk about it?" Maybe that's one reason the talent connected with soap operas tends to move around so much from show to show.

After six months on *Edge of Night,* I was offered more money to write for *All My Children.* That stint lasted until the head writers for *Ryan's Hope,* ABC's newest serial, approached me to ask whether I'd be interested in joining their team. A significant pay raise and the promise of greater professional opportunities made the decision an easy one.

* * *

One day I was in the studio putting some finishing flourishes on that day's script, when an actor scheduled to make his first small appearance didn't show up. Like all TV shows, soaps divide their performers between contract players and bit ones. These minor players usually don't have recurring roles; they're "extras" or "walk-ons" without speaking parts, while others are "under-fives" with fewer than five lines of dialogue.

In a quandary about finding a suitable replacement on such short notice, the director gave me an appraising look. I was the right age, height, weight, and coloring for the character. And I knew his lines, since I had written them. Though I had appeared as a guest on television talk shows, I'd never before been in front of the camera as an actor. But this was an under-five character, and I could easily remember his lines and probably deliver them as well. The cast coached and cajoled me until it was time to go on. I sweated profusely under the hot glare of the studio lights, while a production assistant repeatedly wiped my brow.

Ultimately, I must have given a convincing performance, since the director asked me to return for three more shows. Now that the character had been established, it wasn't prudent to have someone else portray him. I agreed. Imagine my surprise when, two weeks later, I was handed a few pieces of fan mail addressed to me in the name of my character!

The show signed me to a small but recurring part for thirteen weeks, and I began my short-lived acting career. I still penned scripts and now also appeared two or three times a week on the air. It was a heady and flattering experience, especially since people on the street assumed they knew me . . . or, at least, the character I played.

* * *

During the days I acted on the soap, I shared a dressing room with a castmate. Tony was in his early twenties, too, and like me, he had been a teacher before getting involved in the soaps. Slim and perennially tan, his dark, clean-cut looks and dazzling smile had been parlayed into plenty of work as a model. By arranging magazine interviews and encouraging a supportive fan club, his manager had orchestrated a major publicity campaign for him.

As I sat slumped in my dressing room chair, removing the stage makeup after a day's shooting, Tony came in. "You look bushed," he said, slapping me cavalierly on the back. "I bet a good massage would help."

He began to knead the nape of my neck, removing its tight knots and tension. "Got any plans tonight?" he then asked, wanting to know if I was interested in going out on the town with him.

We started with dinner—grilled cheese and bacon sandwiches washed down with red wine—at his midtown apartment, a typical Manhattan high-rise with a small living room, smaller bedroom and galley kitchen. After eating, he excused himself to go to the bathroom.

"What do you think I should wear? Which looks better?" he called from his bedroom, while I waited for him to return to the living room. "Let me see," I answered, making my way to the bedroom.

Tony evidently had taken a quick shower and was standing next to the bed, clad only with a towel tied around his waist. As I walked toward the bed, I stole a glance at his body. He was tall, about six feet two, smooth, had a flat stomach, big biceps and great definition. A deep, flattering tan enhanced his unblemished coloring.

Moving behind me, Tony good-naturedly placed his arms around my shoulders. He turned me around and pressed himself against me. With his towel between us, which he quickly loosened and let drop, I could feel him press against me. Tony took my face in his hands and forced his tongue into my mouth as his lower extremity propelled itself against my groin.

Believing that my attraction to men was purely physical, I refused to kiss or be kissed. Guys didn't kiss each other; it was too emotional, I felt. So I pulled back and disengaged myself.

"You're married, aren't you?" he later inquired, as we waited in the rain for a taxi. Obviously, he already knew the answer, since he continued before I could respond. "That's okay, I know plenty of guys who like it both ways. Don't misunderstand, I think women are great and I really love 'em. I just haven't met many who know what it takes to please a man."

Tony was right on that account.

Guys grow up pretty much pleasing themselves. They know where to touch, what feels really good, and how to milk their anatomies for maximum pleasure. Sex with women is quite different—especially these days with females expecting their own satisfaction, pillow talk, lots of long foreplay, and at least one orgasm before opening up to their men.

Yet, I did love my wife in a tender and caring way. I'd never before been unfaithful to Barbara, and this was the closest I'd come to committing adultery . . . with another man. Working with some of the world's most beautiful people, I had plenty of chances to cheat and lots of temptation which I'd never given into before now. Tony had drawn a distinction between sex and love, rationalizing that one had little to do with the other. Barbara satisfied my needs for a nurturing relationship; but I had desires that she could never fulfill.

I justified my encounters with other men as just that: stray spikes on an otherwise straight and healthy heart line.

* * *

Tony and I spent about two hours at Studio 54, one of the hottest clubs in the city. The fact that we were ushered in while others waited, begging entrance in line, reflected my fifteen minutes of fame. Looking at his watch at eleven o'clock, he wanted to know if I was ready to move on.

"Where to?" I asked.

"Have you ever been to the baths?" he replied, matter-of-factly.

The Club Baths of New York were sandwiched between brownstones on the Lower East Side of Manhattan. You rang the bell at the downstairs entrance and waited for an electric eye to scan you before buzzing you in. A lobby led to a locked door, before which was a window where you registered with the receptionist . . . a slight, older man whose ill-fitting toupee couldn't conceal the ravages of time on his forehead and around his squinty eyes.

"Have you been here before?" he asked me. I shook my head, and he handed me a form to fill out while asking for my driver's license.

Scanning the small print at the bottom of the form, I noticed a statement that really unsettled me: *"By signing this form, I acknowledge that I am a homosexual and that I'm aware homosexual activities occur here—which neither offend me nor violate any of my rights."*

Never before had I been asked or required to make such an absolute confession. Scared about the potential ramifications of signing my name to the document, I quickly scribbled a signature in illegible penmanship and handed the clipboard back to the attendant, who told me my license would be returned when I left.

"Do you want a room or a locker?" he asked, pushing a towel through the window.

"Take a locker," said Tony. "We won't be here that long."

Rooms were for folks wanting privacy, cubicles where they could indulge their fantasies without onlookers. Lockers were fine if you just wanted a place to leave your clothes and didn't mind being watched by others. Tony and I slipped out of our street clothes and wrapped the white threadbare towels around our waists. "Why don't you take a look around and then meet me downstairs in the steam room?" he suggested.

Whoever coined the term "den of iniquity" had been to the Club Baths. Its third and top floor was devoted entirely to the private rooms behind whose doors passersby could hear the guttural grunts of fast and furious, impassioned activity. More cubicles surrounded the second floor lockers, adjacent to which were some showers and a series of open toilet stalls. Behind the locked door past the first floor reception hallway, several jocks were working out in a gym with free weights, Nautilus machines, and some Universal equipment.

Peopled by a dozen or so guys wearing bathrobes, towels, or their birthday suits, a sprawling lounge area completed the first floor's layout amid frayed couches grouped helter-skelter, two color television sets, various pinball machines, and a cash bar.

The anus of the club—and its hub of activity—was found in the bowels of the building. Misty smoke arose from the hot tubs and steam baths, permeating the air so pungent with the sour smell of sex. Wandering through a yellow bricked road, I observed men—white, black, Latino and Asian—flagrantly fornicating.

I pushed my way out of the steam-room doors into a labyrinth leading in and out of nooks, crannies, and crevices where desperate, solitary men lay awaiting anonymous partners to pass their way and service them. The meandering maze ended in a dimly lit chamber where about two dozen guys were banging each other, frantically going at it in an indiscriminate orgy.

The raging revelry made me sick to my stomach. Groping my way back to the lockers, I ripped the towel off my waist and quickly dressed. I ran to the exit, grabbed my driver's license, and took deep gulps of the air outside. My heart beating a mile a minute, I hailed a cruising taxi and headed back to my hotel room.

I never found Tony—nor did I want to—and had abandoned him there inside.

* * *

Shamed by my venture into the soft white underbelly of Gotham's decadent gaiety, which seemed to frame a life of narcissism shared by too many celebrities, I realized I couldn't go back. I'd experienced enough of this hedonistic, self-serving lifestyle to know that it wasn't for me. Nor, after my brush with greatness, could I go back to teaching.

As I headed home in the new BMW purchased for my monthly treks to and from New York, I tried to make some sense of my life, but nothing seemed to fit. I lit up a joint and crossed the New Jersey Turnpike onto one of the twin spans of the Delaware Memorial Bridge.

Suddenly, my heart began to beat uncontrollably. I gripped the steering wheel for dear life, certain that I'd pass out, lose control, and careen off the bridge's guardrails into the swirling water below. Horns honking behind me, I stopped the car and got out to swallow some fresh air and attempt to shake off my hysteria.

At least a dozen times during the rest of the way home, I had to pull off onto the shoulder of the road to clear my head from the recurring nightmare that relentlessly pursued and attacked me. Was I having a heart attack? Had the drugs I'd ingested over the past decade finally conspired into some lethal concoction that was driving me insane? Or was I simply having a "bad trip," a bummer of an experience from some rotten pot?

I never knew.

Doctors diagnosed the problem as an anxiety disorder caused by some sort of chemical imbalance.

They didn't know how or why these "panic attacks" occurred—or why they began when they did—but, in addition to a neurological evaluation, the physicians alternately prescribed Valium, Librium, Ativan, Elevil, Xanax and Prozac . . . one or the other of which I've taken to this day.

14

Soap Box

Following the revelations on my last trip to New York, a letter addressed to me arrived by certified mail within a week of my return. The return address indicated Anthem Press, a publishing company located off Fifth Avenue on Eighteenth Street in Manhattan's warehouse district.

The single-page letter was from Murray Bruckman, an entrepreneur who owned a printing company; he said he got my name and address from Newspaper Enterprise Association, the firm that syndicated my weekly soap opera column. Bruckman produced several of the periodicals marketed by Publishers Clearing House and knew their executive decision-makers well. Anti-trust laws prohibited PCH from owning any of the publications it promoted, but the company was fantastic at marketing and had its fingers on the pulse of what would sell. An arrangement had been agreed upon whereby Bruckman—based on PCH input—created sample issues of new periodicals, which Publishers Clearing House then test-marketed.

In his letter, Bruckman proposed creating a magazine aimed at soap opera fans. He'd be the publisher, and I'd be contracted to serve as its editor. In addition to forming a new corporation in which we'd be 50-50 owners, Bruckman would give me a budget for each issue from which I could hire writers, artists and photographers . . . as well as pay myself a salary.

BRUCE H. JOFFE

About twenty monthly publications catering to the interests of soap opera aficionados already crowded the newsstands, but all were fan magazines devoted to covering the "three deadly Ds" of daytime drama—the stars' diets, dates, and decors—with such provocative headlines as "Why I'll Never Marry an Actor," "My Favorite Recipe for Anchovy Pancakes," and "How I Decorated My Apartment in Balsa Wood."

To be competitive, we'd have to include some gossip, but our vision for *The Soap Box* was "The Newsmagazine of Daytime Drama," focusing more on the stories and less on the stars. Ironically, the tabloid would be a serious publication that treated soap opera viewers as intelligent people who wanted to learn more about life and relied on the soaps as their crystal ball. Bridging the fictional television stories to factual, real-life information, we'd critically analyze the storylines for relevance, authenticity, and verisimilitude.

I was able to write and instinctively knew I could take 48 blank pages and create a solid, stimulating, and well-designed magazine.

* * *

Working from home was a mixed blessing. With three television sets playing simultaneously to capture the doings on all thirteen soaps—this was before VCRs—and a part-time secretary to help me, there wasn't enough room to stretch my legs, let alone to pace creatively in our tiny third bedroom, which had been turned into a cramped office.

Real estate was booming, and even Manassas was growing by leaps and bounds. Double-digit inflation worked to our advantage: We sold our cozy townhouse for a tidy profit and purchased a larger, four-level one where I converted the basement into a fully-equipped office.

On the third Wednesday of each month, I'd leave Manassas and fly to New York (I no longer would drive) and stayed through Sunday, finishing work on our current issue. I stayed with the Bruckmans at their Fifth Avenue duplex facing Central Park, next door to the Guggenheim Museum. Murray's chauffeur would take us downtown every morning and return each evening at six. I was wined, dined, and cradled in the lap of luxury. Everything truly appeared to be coming up roses: In just six months, Publishers Clearing House generated over 300,000 subscriptions for us.

I was thrilled but a bit apprehensive about how well things were going, and anxiously waited for the other shoe to drop.

Sure enough, it soon did.

* * *

In June, I didn't receive a paycheck from Bruckman for the work I had done and assigned to others in April. I waited a week and then called him. He wasn't in, I was told, but would call me back. He didn't. A week later, I called again. This time, he was on the phone and would get back to me. He didn't. By the third week, several of the people to whom I owed money for their services had started to call and I was becoming nervous.

I continued to work on *The Soap Box* and make my monthly trips to New York City. Bruckman was never around, and his flunkies couldn't—or wouldn't—answer my questions or tell me what was going on.

Writers, photographers, and artists who had accepted assignments in good faith were pestering me, threatening to take legal action if they weren't paid. Since I authorized their assignments, the buck stopped on my desk, and I had to do something quickly.

By now, Murray Bruckman had withheld three months of payments from me. It was bad enough that I owed others about $20,000 for the work they'd performed, but I was close to broke and wouldn't be able to make my next mortgage payment.

I tried contacting Bruckman again . . . to no avail. In desperation, I hopped on a plane to pay him a visit in person. He was in and even acknowledged me.

"How're ya doing, kid?" he coughed, puffing away on one of the unfiltered Chesterfields he chain-smoked. "Come on in. The lawyer and I were just talking about you."

Bruckman wanted to sell *The Soap Box*, for a considerable profit, to another publisher. But, first, he wanted to buy me out so that all company stock would be his. I had no idea how much he'd receive from the sale of the publication; he offered me $25,000 . . . leaving just $5,000 after I'd disbursed the money owed to others.

"That's highway robbery," I fumed, assessing the confident slab of a man who sank heavily into a creaking old office chair with a self-satisfied smirk on his thin lips.

"Take it or leave it," he growled.

"And if I don't?"

"Then I suggest you get yourself a good lawyer."

"You're a son of a bitch, you fat bastard," I yelled. "Go to hell."

I consulted a reputable attorney who informed me of my rights.

Yes, I had a good case. Litigation, however, could cost up to $50,000, and it might take several years to resolve the matter. Did I have the money? Evidently not. The lawyer's advice? Take the money and learn a hard lesson: Be more careful before dealing with independent venture capitalists. Bruckman himself had said he wanted to "go in skinny and come out fat."

That's exactly what he did.

Returning to Manassas, I paid off all the outstanding obligations I had incurred for the magazine . . . made three mortgage payments . . . put a few bucks in the bank . . . and filed my claim for unemployment compensation.

I then indulged myself in a well-deserved nervous breakdown.

15

TRICKS OF THE TRADE

For weeks, I didn't get out of bed, except to eat, and watched endless reruns of *Star Trek* and *I Love Lucy*. I loved Lucy but could care less about the soaps. Barbara was compassionate and considerate, at least for the first few weeks, but soon began to lose her patience. "Isn't it about time you started looking for a job?" she'd ask. "You've only got three more months of unemployment, and I can't support us by myself."

Washington is home to the government and trade associations. The help-wanted classifieds advertised few openings for consumer magazine editors; no jobs for soap-opera writers or actors were listed. Barbara suggested I place a position wanted ad, which I did; it ran four consecutive Sundays without a single response.

"How about this one?" she asked, pointing to an ad seeking professional résumé writers on a contractual basis. Writing aptitude was essential, but no experience was required and training would be provided. The job paid $10 an hour. I called, cranked out my own résumé, and went in for an interview. They hired me immediately, teaching me tricks of the trade in preparing commanding chronological and functional résumés, along with the government's Standard Form 171. The résumé company charged clients $30 per hour, paid me $10, and retained $20.

Barbara wondered why I couldn't start my own résumé business.

I placed an ad on the front page of each Sunday's *Washington Post* employment advertising section and our phone soon began to ring. People responded well to the idea of a flat fee for this service and were genuinely impressed by the work I did for them. It was honest work, and I was meeting some interesting people whose lives I delved into and learned to organize or restructure, at least on paper.

* * *

Two of the people I met, Tom and Rosie Greene, would become close friends with Barbara and me. Tom was a driven attorney who worked for the Federal Communications Commission. Obviously in need of a haircut to turn his side-parted sixties' style into a more with-it look, he hated his job and wanted a résumé which could open doors to opportunities in private practice before becoming what he called "one of the walking dead." An attractive brunette courtesy of Elizabeth Arden, Rosie was a buxom nutritionist who looked a little like Barbara. She needed a vita to accompany the research papers she submitted to professional journals.

The Greenes lived less than a mile away, and the four of us got together often. We went to movies, played Scrabble or poker, and ate out frequently. Rosie was intrigued by my wife's eccentric eating habits and confided to me that she considered Barbara a "medical miracle." At the very least, warned Rosie, some of Barbara's vital systems were certain to shut down. How could they survive without better nutrition?

It was Tom who was responsible for finding me a nine-to-five job. One Sunday afternoon he called, asking if I'd seen the *Washington Post* help wanted section yet. I hadn't, so he read me an ad which had caught his eye:

SQUARE PEG IN A ROUND HOLE

DIRECTOR OF COMMUNICATIONS—Leading producer of instructional television programming for children seeks experienced editor familiar with entertainment field. Teaching background and experience in curriculum development preferred. Great opportunity for the right person: excellent salary, outstanding benefits, and interesting environment working with a dynamite ensemble of talented performers.

Wow! Obviously, they were looking for me. After reviewing my résumé and cover letter, it took three sets of interviews for the Children's Television Network to agree.

With the security of health insurance and a year's worth of wages, Barbara and I soon figured it was about time to start thinking about children of our own.

16

THE BEST-LAID PLANS

Like so many children of the '50s grown up in the '60s, Barbara and I fully expected that our lives could be systematically ordered and managed howsoever we chose. Interesting, well-paying jobs and two incomes had enabled us to afford a home, nice furnishings, some travel . . . and now, perhaps, a baby (or two). We'd arrived, successfully, at our late twenties—the perfect time, we reasoned, to begin our own family.

As it turned out, we soon were to learn that having a baby often can be a gamble demanding a substantial investment of faith, perseverance, and money.

Even the best-laid plans often don't always work out the way they're conceived.

* * *

Clinically speaking, they call you "infertile" when, after one year of trying, you remain childless. Such an ugly word. We shunned its implications, preferring to believe that, for us, having a baby was only a matter of time . . . and more intensified effort.

Barbara's gynecologist suggested some routine tests to determine the problem. Was it hormonal? Perhaps her tubes were blocked. Did she have endometriosis, a scarring of the uterine lining? Most important, was she producing any eggs? For my part, was I producing enough sperm and were they sufficiently mobile? What kind of underwear did I wear? Jockey shorts and briefs could overheat the scrotum and damage or reduce sperm, so the doctor advised me to stick to less form-fitting boxers.

I scheduled a visit to a urologist who'd rate the level and performance of my own contributions. The test results showed that I was in fine shape. As for Barbara, the only obvious problem was that she wasn't ovulating normally. Diagnosis: anovulatory. Prescription: pills to regulate her periods and others to stimulate egg production. Prognosis: good. There was no reason to expect we wouldn't become parents soon.

Two bedside companions—a temperature chart and basal thermometer—joined us, which would be constant reminders of our shared hopes and frustrations.

In all of those months, maybe ovulation occurred once.

Tom and Rosie, who were also having reproduction problems, recommended Dr. George Speck, an OB/GYN who had pioneered techniques to deal with infertility. There was a waiting list to see the doctor; but his new associate, Dr. John Mathis, could see us. We were comforted to learn that Mathis, himself, was a "Speck baby."

Our initial consult lasted more than three hours. After reviewing our medical records, the doctor detailed the logistics of conception and explained why procreation really is a "miracle of birth." So much had to happen, so many support systems had to function simultaneously and cooperate, it was truly a miracle that anyone got pregnant!

A treatment plan was presented, along with a new set of buzz words: There were prolactin tests and estrogen tests and thyroid tests and tests to determine if my sperm and Barbara's cervical mucus were antagonistic.

Our schedule called for the alarm to be set for 5:30 am. Then, following sex before sunrise, Barbara was to insert a plug and rush to the doctor for a post-coital test. She'd have to race back to her school, then on to the hospital that same afternoon for a sonogram, and then back—again—to the doctor for yet another injection.

Month after month, things looked promising. Barbara produced good mucus, temperatures, estrogen levels, and follicles. As she developed all the right symptoms—late periods, morning sickness, weight loss, etc.—we rushed to the hospital for a specialized blood analysis that would tell whether a fertilized egg had attached itself to Barbara's uterine wall.

Had pregnancy occurred?

"Doubtful," said the doctor when we called for the test results. Doubtful? How could a supposedly conclusive test indicate maybe yes, maybe no?

By this time, the peaks and valleys of the temperature chart had begun to measure our emotions, reflecting the ups and downs of our patience toward each other. The baby boom surrounding us didn't help matters much, either. Family and friends continued to call us excitedly to report on their good news. But for us, there were long, drawn-out periods of emotionally draining stress because the hormones Barbara consumed tended to drag what used to be "that time" of the month on forever.

We were thankful that the ordeal, somehow, had strengthened our relationship as we learned about other couples driven apart by the strain and tension.

Ten months had passed since we first consulted an infertility specialist, and after five cycles of therapy, Barbara remained barren. We agreed to one last attempt. This time the treatment cycle would be fortified by mild tranquilizers (to calm us), antibiotics (just in case some unknown germs were conspiring against us), and a glass or two of nocturnal wine (to restore a little romance to the mechanics of our lovemaking).

It didn't work.

One year and $15,000 later, we had little choice but to accept our infertility. In retrospect, it wasn't really that high a price to pay.

17

JEWS AND JESUS

"God wants you to have children," insisted our art director over lunch one day, as I described the painful process we had undergone in our efforts to have a baby. "He promises that you will be blessed more than any other people and that none of your men or women will be childless."

Joel was an eternal optimist and born-again Christian. A ruddy, sandy-haired fellow with a receding hairline maximized by his wife's attempts at kitchen snipping, he brought his Bible to work with him and spent time reading it each day. He flipped it open to Deuteronomy 7:14 in the Old Testament—my people's book, he emphasized. Pushing it my way, he pointed to the passage that unequivocally stated "there shall be no male or female barren among you."

But to whom did this verse refer? Who were the *you* ... these people whom God evidently promised to bless more than any others? Certainly not the Jews!

Jewish people suffer more than any others on earth.

Some of my distant relatives had been killed in the Holocaust, yet my personal experiences with bigotry and bias had been limited to overhearing racial slurs and ethnic epitaphs. A co-worker uttered, "Don't Jew me down" when we negotiated the price of a used dishwasher she was buying from us, and at Bishop Ireton, some disgruntled students resentfully had mumbled "kike," "hymie," or "hebe" when I assigned them less-than-satisfactory grades.

My religious experiences had been few and far between. Their highlight occurred many years ago . . . my *bar mitzvah,* the day I "became a man" and confirmed as a responsible member of the covenant people, according to my religion. But that didn't mean much to me since my *bar mitzvah* was more of a social event; and I finally freed myself from the hated Hebrew lessons, which prepared me to chant my passage from the *Haftorah,* Old Testament readings from the prophets. Apart from an exhaustive series of incantations spoken in Hebrew, a language I never really learned and even more quickly forgot, my Jewish experiences could be summed up in the few times my parents bought synagogue tickets for the High Holidays services or I attended someone else's *bar mitzvah.*

All things considered, for me, Judaism most probably represented a way of life . . . a culture, heritage, and ethical orientation stressing the importance of family, good works, and the motivation to succeed.

Nevertheless, Joel was fascinated by the simple fact that I was Jewish. He worshipped the God of Israel. "My Lord is your Messiah," Joel asserted, saying most Christians tend to forget that Jesus and his disciples were Jewish. According to Joel, real Christianity was Jewish in origin, and many Jews were lately coming to believe in Jesus.

Encouraging me to "let go and let God" deal with the matter of our infertility, he asked whether I had heard of Messianic Judaism.

Vaguely, I recalled the pious rabbis in Jerusalem who were said to be praying and awaiting for the Messiah's return. I also had known about so-called Jews for Jesus who stood on street corners handing out a variety of clever tracts with gospel messages.

I did know there were various forms of Judaism.

SQUARE PEG IN A ROUND HOLE

While my own family and Barbara's belonged to the Conservative branch, I basically considered myself an agnostic: God helps those who help themselves. Religions are essentially alike, I assumed. They all have some good points and can help people to lead worthwhile lives. If you need a religion to help you do that, I guess there's nothing wrong with it. But I didn't. I did well enough for myself. Besides, notwithstanding my Bishop Ireton encounter with New Testament verities, certain fundamental beliefs had been ingrained in me.

For one thing, I told Joel, Jews believe in one God—not three. I hardly remember any of my religious training, but I'll never forget the most elementary prayer of Judaism: *Sh'ma Israel, adonai elohenu, adonai echad.* Hear, O Israel, the Lord, thy God, the Lord is one.

For another, Jews don't believe in someone else dying for their supposed sins. Jewish people don't believe in human sacrifice. We don't believe in sin, either, at least not the Christian idea about some original sin we inherited from Adam and Eve because a snake had bamboozled her.

Doing something wrong, sinning, in that we can believe. But the idea of someone else dying for our sins is anathema to us. We don't need a middleman. We pray directly to God, not to any saints or to some virgin.

As I ticked off the reasons why Jews reject Christianity, it suddenly dawned on me that Judaism defines itself more by what it *doesn't* believe than what it does. But Joel had hit upon a chord that somehow rang true. Perhaps it was the result of our battle with infertility, or maybe it was something else more essential. Whatever the reason, Barbara and I agreed that something was missing in our lives.

And maybe, just maybe, that something was religion.

* * *

We decided to investigate our options, beginning with the religion into which we were born. Friday night and Saturday morning "synagogue shopping" at Sabbath services conducted by various congregations became part of our weekend routine. Orthodox Judaism was foreign to our parents and to us, so we began by visiting several Conservative synagogues. Little had changed since we attended these services during our youth, and we left feeling empty, unfulfilled by the strange language, rotes, and rituals to which these synagogues subscribed.

Next, we visited a couple of Reform Jewish congregations. It was strange to see a choir and an organist—not to mention a female rabbi—in a Jewish setting. After the sermon, congregational debate over whether to publish their new prayer book in a loose-leaf binder to better accommodate additional prayers and worship materials or in a more timeless bound volume seemed quite silly to us. Looking at each other after the service, Barbara and I wondered what the real focus of our religion had become.

Babs Bloomgarten, one of my co-workers, was Jewish but belonged to the Ethical Society. Many of its members were disenfranchised Jews, she said, who had joined the Unitarian Church—a religion without creed or dogma that encouraged its members to use their God-given intelligence to understand the Creator and the purpose of our existence. Services were held Sunday mornings in a contemporary structure near her home, and she invited us to accompany her.

We attended Unitarian church for over a month. Barbara and I felt comfortable there, were impressed by its "extended family" concept which provided a network of support to each other, and found the readings from Erich Fromm's *The Art of Loving* to be intellectually stimulating. But spiritually, the service still left us hungry for soul food. We could hear such secular stuff discussed at almost any civic auditorium.

Joel, meanwhile, continued preaching the gospel to me and persistently attempted to document the link between the Old Testament and the New one in his Bible.

Earthquakes . . . famine . . . wars . . . the energy crunch . . . power shifts in the Middle East . . . blinding technological changes . . . pollution and global

SQUARE PEG IN A ROUND HOLE

warming . . . the nuclear threat . . . the whole confusing swirl of events which is our world: Is there a pattern, a meaning, to all this?

Yes, Joel maintained, they're all part of a detailed scenario announced thousands of years ago by biblical prophets.

According to Joel, in the beginning God created the heavens and the earth. God wanted to establish a kingdom in which people freely sought to worship and enjoy fellowship with their Creator. But man is a proud and arrogant creature who prefers to set his own terms and conditions, even when they deliberately contradict those expressly forbidden by God. A spiritual battle had henceforth ensued, pitting God and goodness against Satan and sin.

God had a battle plan, Joel explained, based upon four simple spiritual laws: (1) God loves us, regardless of our apathy. (2) Because he is holy, sin separates us from God. (3) God provided a way to atone for our sins so that we, once again, could be with him. That way is Jesus. (4) All we have to do is ask God's forgiveness and invite Jesus into our lives as Savior.

"The Scriptures tell us that the life of the flesh is in the blood," Joel concluded. "God accepted the blood of an unblemished animal sacrificed in the Temple as a covering—an atonement—for our sins."

As commanded in the Old Testament laws, however, only sacrifices made in the Temple by a descendent of the high priest were acceptable. The blood covenant based upon animal sacrifice was insufficient and temporary, since it could never really restore man to his original standing in which Adam related to God.

"The prophet Jeremiah tells us about a new covenant that would restore man's connection to God," Joel continued. Holding out his Bible, he asked me to read the passage to which he referred: *Behold the days are coming, says the Lord, when I will make a new covenant with the house of Israel and with the house of Judah—not according to the covenant that I made with their fathers . . . this is the covenant that I will make with them: I will put my law in their hearts; and I will be their God, and they will be my people . . . For I will forgive their iniquity, and their sin I will remember no more.*

This new covenant, Joel maintained, was the entire basis for the New Testament and for his own belief in Jesus. God became flesh in the person of the Messiah with the power to live a sinless life. Under the new covenant, everyone who believes in this Messiah is restored to a right relationship with God because our sins are no longer held against us.

So it all came down to belief in this Messiah. I wondered what made Joel so sure that Jesus was the Messiah. Again he rattled off a litany of Old Testament Scriptures which "conclusively proved," he held, that Jesus, without doubt, was the Messiah.

"Scripture says that the Messiah's ancestry is so specific that only one person in all of history—Jesus of Nazareth—could qualify," claimed Joel. "The Bible says he would be born in Bethlehem and that his ancestry would be reckoned through King David. He would die before the second Temple was destroyed in 70 AD by the Romans. He would be rejected by his own people. He would die by crucifixion yet conquer death."

I must admit, all of this stuff was pretty interesting . . . at least theoretically. But when Joel handed me his Bible and asked me to read aloud this account of the Messiah written by the prophet Isaiah 700 years before Jesus was born, it really caught me off guard and caused me to stop and think seriously about the possibilities:

> *He is despised and rejected by men. A man of sorrows and acquainted with grief. And we hid, as it were, our faces from him. He was despised, and we did not esteem him. Surely he has borne our griefs and carried our sorrows. Yet we esteemed him stricken, smitten by God and afflicted. But he was wounded for our transgressions. He was bruised for our iniquities. The chastisement for our peace was upon him. And by his stripes we are healed. All we like sheep have gone astray. We have turned, every one, to his own way. And the Lord has laid on him the iniquity of us all.*

A smile played across his face as Joel looked intently at me.

"Tell me, Bruce. If Jesus isn't the Messiah, who then is?"

* * *

I was intrigued by the puzzle, this paradox that begged to be solved. Whether or not Jesus really was who his followers believed him to be, I was fascinated by the schism between Judaism and Christianity. If Jesus, his disciples, the apostles and early church, in fact, were Jewish, then what had happened to change things? Originally, gentiles had to accept Judaism in order to become Christians. So why did Jews now have to convert? How did the church become so gentile? Why and when did the Jews reject Christianity? When and why did Christians begin rejecting Jews?

I read everything I could get my hands on, exploring these questions. When I was done, my mind was convinced that Jesus was Israel's promised Messiah, while my heart convicted me that he was who he said he was—our collective redeemer.

Joel invited us to accompany him to a Messianic Jewish congregation in Maryland where Jews who believe in Jesus gathered to worship.

18

Born Again

Beth Messiah met in a junior high school gymnasium. Locking my BMW in the school's parking lot, I noticed bumper stickers affixed to many car fenders: "God Loves Israel" and "Pray for the Peace of Jerusalem" were prominent; but the one I liked best was a bit more humorous: "My Boss Is a Jewish Carpenter."

The sound of music—guitars, drums and electric keyboard—could be heard as we made our way to the gym. A band seemed to be playing rock and roll music, but the accompanying words were distinctly inspirational. Wearing skullcaps and fringed prayer shawls, most of the men were young, well dressed, and extremely lively. Together with the women and children, they clapped their hands and danced around the room, arms and hands lifted in prayerful praise. The merry din contrasted sharply with the more somber, austere atmosphere of the synagogues we had visited recently.

We took our seats in old, standard-issue folding chairs as the service began. The liturgy wasn't much different from traditional synagogues, although it was more upbeat, and a spirit of peace and contentment seemed to have settled over the congregation. The name *Yeshua*—which we soon realized was Hebrew for Jesus—was periodically interspersed throughout prayers, music, and the message delivered by a bearded fellow with sparkling blue eyes who must have been the "rabbi."

When the service concluded, a number of people came by to introduce themselves and greet us. It was a pleasant experience, and we felt welcome and comfortable there. On the ride back to Manassas, Joel asked us what we thought of the worship and how it compared to what we'd seen elsewhere. I was noncommittal, but allowed that I had enjoyed it. Barbara simply nodded.

The following Saturday, Barbara and I returned by ourselves to Beth Messiah. Several of the people we'd met the week before remembered our names and seemed genuinely pleased to see us again. When the service concluded, we responded to the altar call and acknowledged Jesus as our Messiah, Lord, and Savior.

What made us do it? I can't, for sure, say. But Barbara and I knew in our hearts that we'd heard God calling us. So we went.

After the service, we left for lunch with a bunch of the assembly's members who told us more about their beliefs and the synagogue's structure.

I guess you could say that Messianic Jews are more Jewish Christians than Christian Jews. "Judaism was the religion *of* Jesus," maintain Messianic Jews. "Christianity is the religion *about* Jesus." But Christianity, by itself, can't stand as a religion; its roots are in the Jewish concepts of the Bible. Because of ignorance and prejudice, however, most people promote the idea that you must be one or the other—either Jewish or Christian—and that these are mutually exclusive categories.

* * *

Like most new believers, Barbara and I were imbued with a sense of euphoria. We began to read and meditate on the Bible daily, avidly listened to Christian radio broadcasts, and prayed for guidance about literally every aspect of our lives, no matter how trivial (finding a downtown parking spot, what and whom to have over for dinner, how and where to spend our vacation). Privately, I asked God's forgiveness for my wayward ways and pleaded with him to take away my attraction to men. We walked around with silly smiles on our faces and, of course, pestered everyone we met by insisting on telling them about our salvation.

Phil and Belle weren't at all happy about our new beliefs. Naturally, they believed I had brainwashed their daughter into joining a dangerous cult that obviously made a mockery of real Judaism.

Nevertheless, we soon became integrated within Beth Messiah and began to attend its Friday night "prayer and praise" service as well as Saturday morning's more traditional Sabbath service. We quickly learned a new lexicon of holy concepts and jargon.

Not everyone who claims to be a Christian has gone through a *conversion experience* or been *born again*. Many don't even attend *believing* churches. Some are *Fundamentalist,* some *Evangelical,* others *Charismatic,* and yet others are *Pentecostal.*

Charismatic Pentecostals *speak in tongues, bind and loose spirits, cast out demons,* and get *slain in the spirit.* *Secular humanism* and *situational ethics* compromise God's standards, so lots of tightly-knit congregations practice *discipleship* and are into *shepherding,* whereby God *raises* leaders who counsel members of their community. They discourage *spreading bad reports* but are *led* to pray about things for which they have *burdens.*

Our own *covenant group*—about a dozen or so folks who met weekly at each other's homes—had a burden for Barbara and me . . . for our desire to have a baby. Through *intercessory prayer,* they *confessed Scriptures* and *claimed promises* which God supposedly made to his people, such as Deuteronomy 7:14: neither male nor female among us would be barren. Unfortunately, Barbara still didn't get pregnant; instead, she sometimes got her period precisely when the group prayed over her.

"Praise God!" they cried. "That was definitely a *sign* from the Lord," said someone alleged to have the *gift of prophecy*. God wanted us to adopt a child. Had we ever considered adoption? We should *set a fleece* to confirm what God was telling us.

19

ADOPTING PROBLEMS

The adage, "adopt . . . then you'll probably have biological children of your own," didn't comfort us, since, as we quickly learned, adoption couldn't provide a promising alternative. A combination of reliable birth control methods, legalized abortion, and the women's movement—the stigma no longer so prevalent, unwed mothers were now opting to keep their children born out of wedlock—contributed to fewer babies being placed for adoption.

It was possible, we were told, to adopt a handicapped child, but for us, that wasn't acceptable because Barbara dealt with special needs children in her classroom all day long. The demands were too great, we felt, for two working parents to cope with the problems of exceptional children—both the school's and at home.

And so, the search for a healthy child, preferably an infant, began. We compiled a list of adoption agencies and proceeded to make telephone calls. Starting with public social service departments, all informed us that no infants were there to be had. Would we consider serving as foster parents to older adolescents or troubled teens?

Next came the religious-affiliated agencies. We contacted the Jewish Community Center in Rockville, Maryland. We were "lucky," they told us, because their waiting list would close at 40; we were number 38. How long a wait could we expect? About four years!

Catholic Charities periodically had younger children available for adoption; but to be eligible, at least one parent had to be Catholic. Similar requirements were placed by Episcopal Social Services and the Baptist Children's Home. Lutheran Social Services didn't ask our religion, but had no children. Christ Child Society referred us to St. Anne's Infant Asylum which, in turn, sent us back to Catholic Charities.

When we heard of a young, unwed pregnant woman who attended a local church, we contacted her pastor who said he'd be glad to consider us as adoption candidates if we'd become members of his congregation.

A network television program announced that homes were needed for Korean orphans, so we followed instructions and called the American Red Cross. The local chapter hadn't heard about the need or the organization's program and referred us once again to Catholic Charities.

Baltimore's Jewish Community Center, we were told, needed families in which to place exiled Iranian children of Semitic descent. The agency's social worker said she knew nothing about it. She did not tell us to call Catholic Charities.

* * *

Occasional business travels took me to cities all over the United States. Wherever I went, I looked up "Adoption Agencies" (see "Social Services") in the local telephone directories. Somewhere, sometime, somehow, there'd be a child for us, I prayed.

During a trip to Miami, I began the by now routine process anew. The fourth and final number I dialed was answered on the third ring.

"Universal Aid for Children," said a woman's voice with a strong New York accent. "I'm alone in the office and talking long distance on the other phone. Can you wait a few minutes while I put you on hold?" The nasal voice belonged to Lori Kellogg, founder of a non-profit agency dedicated exclusively to international adoptions.

Later, when I met her, I realized how well that voice fit the robust, henna-haired woman whose energies were devoted to destitute children rather than her own social graces.

"I'm sorry to have kept you waiting so long, but I was on an overseas call," Lori apologized. "Now, how can I help you?"

Midway through my lamentation, she stopped me, assuring me that she'd heard it all before from countless other people; still, she seemed interested and genuinely concerned. Since ours was the first out-of-state international adoption they'd encountered, however, we'd have to proceed judiciously by letting the agency's attorney study Virginia's adoption law.

"Don't worry, darling . . . we won't leave you hanging," she said. "If we can't help you, we'll find people who can and put you in touch."

It was off to the library to copy some 20 pages of the Virginia State Code, then waiting and dreading her call with the verdict. Two weeks later, we received our first good news: within certain limitations, the agency could—and would—represent us.

"Lori, you're a saint," I declared before disconnecting.

"No, I'm not," she argued. "You'll soon find out that I'm the one who gives God all of those Excedrin headaches!"

* * *

Since we preferred an infant, and only children from South or Central America were being placed at the time, El Salvador was suggested. Adoptions from that country were relatively the easiest to arrange.

If we thought we had had issues dealing with infertility, a child from El Salvador represented an entirely new set of concerns. The country's internal political chaos already had resulted in thousands of deaths, not just military casualties but innocent women and children. The Salvadoran passport office had been bombed, there were periodic attacks on the U.S. Embassy, and roads were often too dangerous to travel.

"A baby is due to be born within the next two to three weeks," Lori briefed us in February. "If the child is healthy and the mother signs the required consent, the baby is yours!"

Joyously, we began marking off days on the calendar.

Two weeks later, Lori's second call came. "I'm sorry to say," she began, "that the girl still hasn't given birth. But I've just been informed that there's a healthy baby girl, two-months-old, who's available now . . ."

Confessing to each other that, secretly, we each had hoped for a girl, we called Lori back and said that we wanted her. The commitment was made without praying, seeing the child's picture, or even receiving her medical report. These would follow shortly.

As it turned out, we had made the right decision, since, the very next day, we again heard from Lori. The girl we were originally waiting for had given birth; however, she'd decided to keep her baby. But the paperwork for our new foundling in El Salvador was now being processed.

Except there was one problem . . .

*   *   *

"I don't quite know how to tell you this," Lori apologized. "Are you sitting down?" An error in translation had been made somewhere between the Salvadoran attorney's office and the agency's secretary. Muchach*o* was mistaken for muchach*a;* it turned out that our darling little daughter, in fact, was a beautiful baby boy.

Did it matter to us?

We agonized over this new twist of providence. Nothing, thus far, had occurred according to our plan. Instead of our own, we'd be adopting; instead of a newborn, we'd parent a child who'd probably be four or five months before arriving; and now, instead of a girl, we'd be getting a boy.

"Thy will be done," our covenant group prayed, and we decided to go ahead with the adoption. Barring unforeseen circumstances, we could expect to receive our baby in two to four months—possibly sooner.

In the middle of March, we received a passport-size photo of our son and a preliminary medical report from the Salvadoran pediatrician who had examined him. Approximately four months old, he weighed 11 pounds and measured just about two feet. He was found to be in overall good health except for some minor skin eczema on his neck and buttocks.

Lori finally received our baby's official papers on April 20 and rushed them, along with our pre-processed visa petition, to Miami's Immigration and Naturalization Service office for immediate approval. They were cabled that same afternoon to El Salvador. Three days later, our son had his visa appointment at the American embassy in San Salvador. He was cleared for immigration to this country on the following Monday.

On April 27, our baby was escorted from El Salvador on a flight which arrived at 1:30 pm in Miami. Lori Kellogg was on hand to receive him at the airport, where she waited with him three hours for a 4:50 flight into Washington, D.C.

Jonah (né José Elias Rodriguez) arrived at 7:00 pm via an Eastern Airlines flight at National Airport.

But it still wasn't over. There would be post-placement tests to go through with our municipal social service agency while Tom Greene petitioned the Virginia State Court in our behalf for Jonah's adoption. There would be pediatrician visits to arrange, and of course, we'd have to exchange Barbara's basal for a new rectal thermometer.

20

HELL TO PAY

Was it Winston Churchill who once said, "If you're not a liberal when you're 20, you have no heart. If you're not a conservative when you're 40, you have no head"?

Probably not.

No matter. Had Churchill been a Christian and attended the churches I knew, he certainly would have rephrased this standard. Age, stressed these God-fearing Christians, has little to do with one's outlook and orientation. What really counts is whether you're a full-fledged Bible believer. According to their interpretation of the Bible, certain beliefs are irrefutable.

Cigarettes, alcohol, and drugs are bad, since our bodies are supposed to be the temples of God's Holy Spirit. God hates divorce, so woe to anyone who puts asunder what he's joined together. Given that God is the author of all conception and birth, abortion is wrong in almost every circumstance. Sex outside of marriage is verboten. Needless to say, homosexuality is an abomination punishable by excommunication and expulsion . . . if not death.

Freedom of religion vs. separation of church and state. How did I feel about prayer in school? Evolution and creationism? Reproductive rights? Capital punishment? Retribution and restitution? "Are these civil or religious issues?" I asked myself.

My values used to be simple. Live and let live, I believed; I did my thing and let others do theirs.

Registered as a Democrat, I guess you'd have called me a liberal. I was in favor of civil rights, affirmative action, and equal opportunity for minorities, radicals, feminists, gays. I smoked and had enjoyed getting high occasionally. Maybe I was just a coward, but I joined in my college protests when the CIA and FBI attempted to recruit students on campus during the Vietnam era. Sex was a normal and healthy function of the libido, and I had had my share of experiences with other men (and a few with women, too).

But everything now depended on whether the powers-that-be in the religious right deemed certain beliefs or behavior as wrong; i.e., "situational ethics" that compromised the absolute values God had decreed. Honestly, I regretted my mistakes and repented my wrongs, asking God's forgiveness for any sins in thought, word, or deed that may have hurt or offended him, as well as anyone (and everyone) else.

Barbara, however, was becoming increasingly resentful of Beth Messiah's godly intrusion on our private lives. Many of its members were making her feel guilty for continuing to teach and leaving Jonah in day care. Home schooling was best, they believed, and full-time motherhood was God's preferred position for submissive wives.

Unfortunately, neither Barbara nor I was particularly submissive.

* * *

Our relationship had changed, becoming more antagonistic and confrontational. There was a hard and brittle edge now to Barbara, slashing away at her soft and gentle spirit. Jonah had added another variable to our marital equation, and hardships caused by financial pressures at work didn't help matters much, either.

SQUARE PEG IN A ROUND HOLE

Ronald Reagan's new economic policies had hit Children's Television Network hard. Funding was drastically cut for education in general, and instructional television, specifically, was considered frivolous fluff. CTN lost contracts to produce series for the National Endowment for the Humanities and the National Science Foundation. Educational efforts at the state level were significantly restricted, leaving little money for CTN's customers to spend on our programs.

To compensate, CTN cut staff salaries by 10% across-the-board. Two months later, we were furloughed; our workweek was reduced to four days with another cut in pay. Fringe benefits—retirement, health, and disability insurance—were discontinued.

CTN's president, Stanley Friedman, called me into his office for a serious talk after we had missed two paychecks when a few major customers hadn't paid substantial outstanding invoices.

"You know how much I value your work and regret the financial problems we've been having," he began, drumming his swollen fingers on the desk and anxiously shifting his bulk from side to side in the imitation leather chair. "We've stopped producing any new programs and are trying desperately to stay afloat by promoting the materials we already have in inventory."

I nodded, aware that our staff of 37 writers, producers, directors, film editors, and cinematographers had been reduced to six essential administrators and bureaucrats—me being one of them. But my time, too, was coming to an end. That Friday.

Stanley wanted to know if I would consider working as a consultant. I'd be an independent contractor responsible for paying my own taxes and insurance, but I could work from home and set my own hours. The work would pretty much be the same. Plus, I could take on additional clients.

Sure, I said. What more did I have to lose? Except, maybe, our new house.

We'd put a deposit on a beautiful split-level home to be built on a cul-de-sac about a mile from our townhouse. The market was good, and homes were appreciating quickly; our real estate agent was certain our house would sell soon and we'd walk away with about $20,000 to invest in our new place. The single-family home would have four bedrooms, 2.5 baths, a huge family room with fireplace, finished basement, two-car garage, and three skylights. There even was a library for my office and study.

Barbara believed that a new home could bring us back together and repair some of the damage caused by our mutually destructive behavior. Her attitude reminded me of the soap operas, where characters with faltering relationships decide to have a baby in a last-ditch attempt to redeem their marriages. It never worked.

* * *

Fortunately, I gained a new client when one of Beth Messiah's more prominent members asked for my help in editing his newsletter and preparing fundraising appeals.

Saul produced a nationally broadcast radio ministry and was planning to publish the first "kosher" New Testament. He thought my media expertise could help him to publicize it.

I also began teaching courses twice each week at George Mason University, a public educational institution in Northern Virginia. The résumé I'd crafted for Tom Greene had opened the door to a lucrative position at a law firm specializing in telecommunications. Tom augmented his professional credentials by serving as an adjunct professor at the university. Turnabout being fair play, Tom recommended me when his department was seeking a qualified practitioner to introduce courses on public relations and publications management—emerging areas of interest for the school's growing communications curriculum.

Barbara resented the long hours I was putting in and expected me to help more with the housework. Complaining about the distance we had to *shlep* back and forth to Beth Messiah, she began to nag about curtailing our attendance. Unaccustomed to hearing Barbara give orders or make demands, I acquiesced to her wishes. So, as she grumbled more about the congregation's expansive influence over our private life, I agreed to visit another place of worship.

One Sunday, we attended services at a non-denominational church that teachers at Barbara's school attended and highly recommended.

Christian Assembly wasn't a Messianic Jewish congregation, but a few of its members were what we called "completed" or "fulfilled" Jews—Jews who believe in Jesus. The church was closer to home. Like Beth Messiah, it was Charismatic and preached submission to higher authorities. A congregational "pot faith" meal followed services almost every Sunday.

When several members noticed her strange eating habits and questioned me about them, I was embarrassed and Barbara immediately was put on the defensive. Though she now only weighed about 100 pounds, Barbara still insisted on limiting her diet to lettuce, cottage cheese, and dry potato skins. If they weren't available, she just didn't eat.

* * *

I had become familiar by now with the anorexia syndrome and realized Barbara's extreme dieting was symptomatic of a deeper need to be in control. This need to take charge manifests itself in compulsive obsessions and a rebellious spirit. That pretty much described Barbara.

Insecure in her teaching competency, she'd get up early and stay up late to devise relevant lesson plans and creative instructional materials. Each day, the house had to be vacuumed and dusted while, every night, another load of laundry was washed, dried, and folded. A vacuum—we had three, one for each floor—became a standing fixture in our living room.

People invited over for dinner would feel uncomfortable when Barbara brought out the vacuum and began to remove their plates before they had finished eating. Although she played with her food rather than eat it, our pantry, refrigerator, and cabinet shelves overflowed with enough food to feed a starving village.

It was difficult enough coping with her personal extravagances, but Barbara also had begun to project her need to control onto Jonah, now nearly three-years-old. She insisted on feeding, dressing, and disciplining him her way, and we'd wage bitter battles over the best way to raise our child.

Though I resented Barbara's obsessiveness with our son, I hated to fight. Sometimes, I humored her. Rather than standing up for my paternal rights, I tried to hold onto our marriage by avoiding conflict and following my preferred philosophy—life should go through the path of least resistance—and retreated to my study, closing the door behind me.

That, of course, further alienated Barbara who warned me that if I didn't begin to pay more attention to her and less to my work and others, there'd be hell to pay. If her needs weren't fulfilled at home, she threatened to satisfy them elsewhere.

21

SEPARATION ANXIETIES

Barbara stayed home when I went to Wednesday night Bible studies at Christian Assembly; she skipped Sunday services, dropped out of our monthly home group meetings, and did her own thing on Friday nights when I'd go to the church's uplifting prayer and praise services.

She was developing new friendships with people I objected to: teachers and support staff who not only weren't Christians, but free-spirited divorcées and women separated from their husbands. They'd go out dancing and drinking at bars—Barbara still would drink, if not eat—and spend time commiserating in impromptu support groups, talking about their personal problems, and seeking strength or solace through each other's experiences. Barbara also began to get involved in her school's extra-curricular activities. She'd take off, alone, for educational conferences and weekend trade shows.

Noting her absences, Christian Assembly members were concerned about Barbara's wayward ways. They suggested we seek help in steering our marriage back on track, referring us to a large Episcopal church whose resources included a staff of trained biblical counselors.

Andrew, an ordained priest and certified counselor, listened to my story with interest. His black garb and white collar could have been intimidating, but his hospitable blue eyes and charitable smile more than offset his prominent forehead deeply etched with worry lines.

Regarding how I'd handled my wife and our marriage, he said, "You've done things your way. You've done things her way. You've even done things her parents' way. Isn't it about time, now, that you do them God's way?"

God's way meant laying down the law to Barbara, insisting that she rectify her eating habits and become the supportive wife described in the biblical proverbs: *The wise woman builds her home, but with her own hands the foolish one tears hers down,* quoted Andrew, reminding me that *a quarrelsome wife is like a constant dripping on a rainy day; restraining her is like restraining the wind or grasping oil with the hand.*

I admitted my own shortcomings to Andrew and, in the sanctified spirit of his study, confessed my attraction to other men that I thought God had lifted from me when I became a born-again believer. Affirming that, "God loves the sinner, but hates the sin," Andrew gently placed his hands on my shoulders and prayed for me.

As I left his office, he handed me brochures from ministries dedicated to "liberating homosexuals from their affliction."

Since I thought God and I alone would be able to tame these demons, I filed the materials away in a hidden folder buried at the bottom of a desk drawer for reference when and if I should need them.

* * *

Meanwhile, I focused on redeeming what was left of my marriage. Barbara and I celebrated when our townhouse was sold. We had some good days; but, more often, the bad times prevailed. I was getting nervous as the time to close on our old house and settle into our new one approached.

"We need to talk," I told Barbara.

"About what?"

"Us."

"What about us?"

"I need to know if we really have a future together."

"Why?"

"Because if we don't, I need to know now," I said. "We're taking on a major financial commitment with the new house. There's no way I can afford the monthly payments by myself. I'd rather lose our $1,000 deposit now than to move into the new place only to find myself alone."

"Things will work out," she reassured me. "We're going through some rough spots. All marriages have them. If you just leave me alone and stop picking on me so much, we won't fight all the time. I want to move into that new house."

I left it at that.

*   *   *

Three weeks later, we closed on our new house. Unfortunately, a house doesn't make a home, as I learned during the first week in our new nest. I'd returned unexpectedly early from shopping at Hechinger's, where I'd gone to buy some extension cords and switch plates. I had forgotten my checkbook. Barbara didn't seem to be around. But her car was in the garage. I took off my shoes and walked up the steps to the top floor. Our bedroom door was closed, and I could hear Barbara talking on the phone. I tiptoed back downstairs to my study and did something I wasn't proud of. Silently, I picked up the extension.

"Who was that?" asked a male voice. "Did someone pick up the phone?"

"I didn't hear anything," Barbara replied.

"Are you sure *he's* not home?"

"I don't think so. I didn't hear him come in. He said he'd be gone for a couple of hours. He always spends hours at the hardware store. With all his tools and gadgets, you'd think Mr. Fix-it knew what he was doing," she snickered.

"When am I going to see you?"

"I'm trying to work things out. I don't want to leave Jonah alone with him."

"So bring him."

"Are you kidding?"

"No, not at all. I like kids."

"And how am I supposed to explain that to him?"

"That's up to you. I'm sure you'll think of something."

"Maybe I can. Maybe I'll tell him I'm taking Jonah to go with my sister-in-law when she visits her parents in Pittsburgh."

"When's that?"

"In two weeks . . ."

I'd heard enough. Gingerly, I set the receiver back on its hook and sank down into my chair. My head was spinning, my heart was pounding, and my hands were shaking uncontrollably. Fearing I was going to pass out, I reached for my Xanax and swallowed three without any water. Whatever else might have been wrong between us, I never suspected to be cuckolded. I'd assumed that deception wasn't in Barbara's vocabulary, since she was always so concerned about me deceiving her. But the shoe was on the other foot now.

Grasping the arms of the chair, I raised myself up. Firm in my resolve while all my limbs trembled, I crept up the stairs and stood without a sound in front of the locked bedroom door. Barbara was still talking on the phone. I lifted my leg and kicked in the door.

"Get off the fucking phone," I roared.

"What are you doing here?" she asked, placing her hand over the mouthpiece.

"Unlike some people, I live here!"

"I'll have to call you back," she said into the phone, removing her hand. "He just walked in."

"No, she won't," I shouted, grabbing the phone from her and slamming it down.

"Bastard! You're a goddamn bastard."

"And you're a whore," I yelled. "If, for one moment, you think I'm going to let you take my son to go and see some prick on the sly, you're very mistaken."

"Get out!" Barbara yelled. "Get the hell out of here, now!"

"No, you get out. I've had enough of your shit. I should have listened to the advice at church and put my foot down a long time ago. I'm warning you, you're not going to get away with this. You'll never see Jonah again!"

Shrieking like a banshee, Barbara flew from the room, down the steps, and out the front door. Ranting and raving curses, she ran down the street as neighbors came out to see what was happening. I have no idea where she went or what she did. Within an hour, the tranquilizers' calming effect had helped me to settle my seething nerves, and I went to pick up Jonah at his day care center.

* * *

At eight o'clock, the phone rang. I braced myself, thinking it was Barbara.

"What's going on there?" asked Belle, instead.

"I suggest you ask your daughter," I retorted.

"She's called me already three times and sounds like she's having a nervous breakdown. She says you're threatening to take Jonah away from her. Why?"

"Why don't you ask her?"

"I'm asking you. We've always been able to talk, Bruce. Please, tell me what's happening. I'm petrified that Barbara is going to hurt herself. She said something about throwing herself in front of traffic."

Briefly, I sketched the details of what had occurred that day. Belle knew we were having problems, but she had no idea of their magnitude. Evidently, neither did I. While she found it hard to believe that Barbara was having an affair, she promised to reserve judgment until she could confront her. Belle pleaded with me to remain calm and not do anything rash. She was getting into her car and should be here in less than an hour. Alone. Under the circumstances, she felt it best to leave Phil at home, away from us and out of our dispute.

Belle and I stayed up until two in the morning, talking about what had gone wrong with the marriage. Barbara had confided in her mother about how neglected she felt, how frustrated she was with people always focusing on her shortcomings, how much she needed more positive reinforcement, acceptance, and affirmation. But she hadn't said anything about being involved with another man. That was news to Belle.

Barbara never came home that night. Belle slept in the guest room. When I left the next morning to consult with Saul about an advertising campaign we were planning to launch, Belle camped out at the house to wait for Barbara. Sometime that morning, she returned. I have no idea what Barbara and Belle discussed, but when I got home that afternoon, they both were sitting around the kitchen table.

Belle had tears in her eyes, which were fluttering a mile a minute. Staring resolutely down at the table, she wouldn't or couldn't look directly at me. Barbara, however, returned my look with a scornful glare and an announcement.

"I'm moving out in two weeks with Jonah," she declared, her teeth clenched and jaw firmly set. "You can try to fight me over custody if you want, but I've consulted a lawyer, and he says you have no chance in hell of stopping me or getting Jonah. Despite what you may think, the courts here favor mothers in custody cases. And, whatever else you can say about me, I'm still a damned good mother!"

* * *

Apart from some periodic outbursts, an uneasy truce settled over our household for a short time. Barbara and I stayed out of each other's way, as she tagged the furniture and furnishings she planned to take with her. Though she spoke with her parents several times each day, they never said anything to me. Still waters run deep, and blood is thicker than water.

Six weeks after we moved into our new house, Barbara and Jonah moved out. Padding around the empty house now devoid of two-thirds of my life, I wondered how I'd meet the monthly mortgage and hefty child support payments stipulated in our legal separation agreement.

The Lord giveth and the Lord taketh away. Blessed be the name of the Lord.

22

Temptation

Barbara's parents closed ranks behind her and totally rejected me. I was persona *non grata* as far as they were concerned. Following scriptural principles, a couple of people from the church offered to go with me to confront Barbara and bring her behavior to Phil and Belle's attention. But her parents wouldn't hear of it. Nor would they accept my calls.

My folks, however, wanted to hear everything and were frustrated by my silence. Never particularly thrilled with Barbara, they always had held her first marriage against her. "Once, shame on her; twice, shame on you," they wagged when we first announced our plan to wed, echoing words I had heard before. And, although they had accepted and loved Jonah, they were positive Barbara's barbaric eating habits were the real reason we couldn't give them biological grandchildren. They sent me a plane ticket to visit them in Florida where they dispensed their advice: don't move.

Do whatever was necessary to hold onto the house, they cautioned. Who knew what the future would hold? Maybe I'd meet someone else and remarry. Perhaps (God forbid!) Barbara and I would reconcile. Whatever might ultimately happen, I should stay put in the new house. It would be stupid to sell it. Would I ever again be able to afford another one as nice?

My parents weren't the only ones offering advice. While in Florida, I visited Lori Kellogg, an astute individual who surprised me with her candid insights. From the moment she'd met her, Lori knew Barbara had problems. Anyone who ate like that and lived for the vacuum needed to clean up her act.

Given the circumstances, my Christian friends had their own ideas about what was going on and how I should react. Beth Messiah and most of the gang at Christian Assembly were certain Satan was testing me. I shouldn't give in to temptation. Instead, I was to set a place at the table for Barbara every night (hah!) and claim the promise that she would come to her senses, repent, and return home a changed person. Other, less parochial Christians looked at things differently. By committing adultery, which she freely admitted, Barbara had broken the marriage covenant. Even the Bible said I was free to divorce. What about that?

I was pulled this way and that, unsure of what God wanted from me, from Barbara, from us. I consulted Andrew, again, at his Episcopal church.

Andrew took a moderate approach. Barbara had committed a sin and needed to repent. She had to seek professional help to deal with her eating disorder. And, together, we required marriage counseling.

As Virginia law precluded me from doing anything for another twelve months, even if I wanted to, Andrew suggested I "take a vacation" from the world to spend more time with God. He encouraged me to memorize and meditate upon I Corinthians 13, verses which seal so many wedding vows:

Love is patient, love is kind. It does not envy, it does not boast, it is not proud. It is not rude, it is not self-seeking, it is not easily angered, it keeps no records of wrongs. Love does not delight in evil but rejoices with the truth. It always protects, trusts, hopes, perseveres. Love never fails.

As I left, Andrew asked me about my other "problem." I shook my head and shrugged, taking leave.

* * *

BRUCE H. JOFFE

It had been a number of years since I shared my space with strangers. But to afford my home, I would have to eat humble pie and learn to compromise. I placed an ad in the local newspapers for roommates.

Over a dozen callers responded. Several questioned my policy about boyfriends, girlfriends, and overnight guests. Though I'd specified "professionals only," assorted riff-raff and drifters who worked periodically came by to inspect my property. All were more impressed with the home site than I was with them. Finally, I accepted a month's security deposit and agreed to subdivide my home with two guys in similar predicaments. Both were respectable, gainfully employed, and could identify with my situation.

Each of my roommates paid me $350 a month rent, including utilities, and I was able to manage the mortgage. Business was growing, too. In addition to Saul and Children's Television Network, two associations had bolstered my client roster.

Angela Fletcher, a slightly older and delightfully caustic acquaintance I'd met through an association I joined for public relations professionals, hired me to produce an annual report for the non-profit organization whose communication department she headed.

A printing association contracted with me to handle its monthly newsletter and press releases, along with promoting its annual convention and writing copy for membership recruitment campaigns.

"Crap-cranking," I called it.

Impressed by my portfolio, personal experience, and Spanish language skills, an international adoption agency that had advertised in the *Washington Post* for freelance public relations support retained me to develop marketing brochures, newsletters, and press releases.

George Mason University then asked me to teach another course that semester. On Tuesdays I taught Principles of Public Relations, followed by Case Studies in Public Relations on Thursdays.

I looked forward to my Thursday class, not just because I was more attuned to its subject matter and content, but because of the students. There were 35 upper-level communication majors enrolled, and many were both attractive and attentive.

Flattered by the crushes several cute co-eds obviously had on their professor, I enjoyed surveying the good-looking students in my class who followed me with their looks, scribbling notes and transcribing my words.

Craig, in particular, had caught my eye.

I guess everyone has someone who triggers his or her shotgun; for me, that person was definitely Craig McAllister. Tall, dark, and incredibly virile, Craig was cocky and often challenged me in class. He would wait until the rest of the students had left after our sessions concluded and then swagger to the front of the classroom. His shirt casually unbuttoned, I'm certain Craig was subconsciously flirting as he asked questions that had little or nothing to do with the course or our defined syllabus.

Backslider.

That's Christian terminology for someone who falls off the holiness wagon. I hoped God had taken away my attraction to other men. Maybe he did, for a time, but it was back with a vengeance. It was my cross to bear, I supposed. I couldn't help looking or indulging myself in little fantasies. As long as I didn't act on my desires, however, I convinced myself there was nothing so wrong with having them. Was it my fault the devil knew my weaknesses and tickled my Achilles heel?

"Get behind me, Satan!" I commanded each morning in prayer, determined to confront and conquer this test of my faith. I decided to begin dating, contrary to Andrew's advice.

It was therapeutic, medicinal, I assured myself.

23

Fellowship

An axiom of Charismatic Christianity is to seek fellowship where you are fed. It was difficult enough remaining at Christian Assembly, where well-meaning members treated me with compassion but felt awkward around me. They didn't know what to say, and what not to say, about my marriage difficulties. I was the odd man out and, though they tried to be sensitive, I felt alienated and embarrassed by my social stigma as an outcast.

By referring me to another church for help, the leaders of Christian Assembly acknowledged their inability to deal with my dilemma. Thanks to Andrew's counseling, spiritually, I now was "being fed" at All Saints Episcopal Church. So I transferred my membership there. My social life soon began to revolve around church, although other friends tried to fix me up on blind dates.

Angela Fletcher had recently remarried and knew lots of people from Parents Without Partners. A queen bee and social butterfly, she loved to entertain with theme parties. I was to be the theme of her first summer bash.

24

HUMPING AND THUMPING

The first woman I dated during my separation from Barbara was Debbie Berger, a social worker employed by the international adoption agency I now represented. Tall and well proportioned, Debbie had long, streaked hair and could flash a smile that stopped traffic. Debbie had been going with a doctor for over six years, but he still hadn't popped the question. She was losing patience. We worked together on my assignments to promote the agency. Rather than battle traffic from downtown Washington, where she worked, to Manassas, where I lived and worked, we would have dinner together in the city.

Eating out had become quite a fixation for me. For the first time in ages, I was sampling cuisines other than salad bars. I enjoyed breaking bread with lovely women and found something almost erotic about the social tableau. Later, during therapy, I came to realize that a measure of my interest in a given partner would depend on how and what she ate. After all those years of cottage cheese and dry potato skins, I craved companionship with meat and mashed potatoes.

Debbie and I spent many hours together, getting to know each other quite well. As business turned to friendship, I genuinely came to like her. We laughed a lot, played silly games together, and began to confide in each other. Soon, our perfunctory hugs and kisses good-bye on the cheek became somewhat serious.

Naturally, we reached a critical juncture in our relationship. It was fish or cut bait, time to consummate our relationship and sleep together.

Debbie offered to come to Manassas and spend the weekend. Friday night, we went to eat at an Italian restaurant and then saw *Terms of Endearment* at a nearby cinema. Returning home, Debbie took her bag into my bathroom to brush her teeth and get ready for bed. I was already in bed, stripped to my underpants, when she emerged wearing a lacy negligee. Debbie pulled down the covers and quickly slipped in next to me, her arm gently brushing my right shoulder.

I placed my hands on her face, cupping her cheeks. We kissed. My hands moved on to explore the territory, tracing and caressing the contours of her soft, supple skin. Debbie's nipples were hard, and she moaned as I inched farther south. Quickly, my hands retreated to more comfortable turf. Fingering a nipple with my right hand, my left tugged her negligee up and off as she used both hands to grasp my underpants and pull them down. Circling each areola, my tongue came across an alien intruding on the hallowed terrain. Focusing my vision, I noticed a long, lone hair growing from Debbie's bosom; for some reason, it turned me right off, arresting my manhood and putting it uncomfortably at ease. Talk about poor timing.

"I'm sorry," I apologized, rolling over. "I haven't been with another woman since Barbara, and I guess I'm out of practice. Maybe, unconsciously, I feel guilty. Even though we're legally separated, technically we're still married. I suppose I'm hung up about committing adultery and violating the seventh commandment."

We hadn't talked much about religion. Although not observant, Debbie was Jewish and knew that I believed in Jesus. Since my beliefs never before had infringed on our relationship, that side of my life had gone relatively unspoken.

She kissed me tenderly, spooning herself to my side. "It's nothing to worry about," she yawned before drifting asleep. "We'll have plenty of opportunities to work everything out."

* * *

Over the next few months, we spent many an evening together in each other's arms. Indeed, practice made perfect and I was usually able to perform to our mutual satisfaction. When I did have difficulty rising to the occasion, I closed my eyes and fantasized about Craig McAllister. Debbie never suspected.

My roommate's bedroom was directly below mine, and he would jocularly joke about all the racket made by our humping and thumping and the bed's creaking springs. I felt as though I'd been awarded the Boy Scouts' newest merit badge.

Our six-month anniversary, if that's what you'd consider it, occurred over the Christmas holidays. To celebrate, we planned a big holiday bash with friends—some mine, others hers—invited to join in the festivities. Over 100 people from each of our social circles attended, including members of Beth Messiah, Christian Assembly, and All Saints—some of whom I hadn't seen in many months. Since we began dating, I had spent more time with Debbie and much less at church.

I was really looking forward to seeing Cassie, a photographer and television producer for the Christian Broadcasting Network. We'd met at Beth Messiah and became very good friends. Not particularly pretty in the conventional sense, Cassie was beautiful, though, in spirit and soul. If I could choose a sister, it would be her. We both worked with the media—I in public relations and she in public affairs. Though Cassie was a solid Christian who'd spent the last two years covering news for her network from Israel, she had a deprecating wit, and "Messianic maniacs" were a favorite target of her light-hearted sarcasm.

For some reason, Cassie wasn't her usual outgoing self at the party. Quiet and withdrawn, she took charge of the music instead of making her own merry sounds. Concerned, I pulled her aside.

"Are you all right? Is something bothering you?" I asked.

"I need to talk to you," she replied. "Is there anyplace quiet?"

We went up to the bedroom, where she sat on the edge of the bed. Taking my hand, she pulled me down into a sitting position facing her.

"What is it?" I questioned her. "Is it me? Did I do something to offend you?"

"It's not me you're offending. That I could deal with. It's much worse. You're offending God."

"What do you mean?" I asked, knowing full well what she was going to say.

"You know that I love you. Not only as a brother in the Lord, but as a real brother. I just can't stand by silently and watch you defile the holiness that God expects of you. We're supposed to conform to a higher standard, but you're behaving just like everyone else, and it hurts me to watch.

"If Jesus returned tomorrow," she continued, "do you honestly think he would take you with him? You've become way too worldly, forsaking God for passions of the flesh. Promise me you'll pray about this and let the Holy Spirit guide you. I'm looking forward to spending eternity in heaven together and would hate to be there without you!"

Sunday morning, I went to church and prayed fervently about the matter. I confessed my sins "in thought, word, and deed" for what I'd "done and left undone" and left church feeling somewhat better, if not resolved, in any decisions.

At home, I packed for another quick trip to visit my folks in Florida.

The five sunny days flew by in a flash. Soon it was December 31, time to return home. Not only was it New Year's Eve, but Debbie's birthday fell on that day. I'd given her a key to my house, and she would be waiting for me, expecting to bring the New Year in with a bang while we toasted the dual occasion.

As I walked across the airport tarmac to board the plane, I sensed trouble with the spirit of God. Cassie was right. God wasn't happy about my relationship with Debbie . . . and I knew he wanted me to end it.

Debbie was looking out the window as I pulled the car into the driveway just before midnight. She ran outside to greet me. Mechanically, I kissed her on the cheek and put my hand on her shoulder as we walked to the front door.

"You can't stay," I apologized, placing my luggage in the foyer.

"Why? What's wrong? What happened in Florida?" she responded. "Talk to me! You owe me an explanation. What's going on?"

"I can't talk about it now; I just need to be alone. We'll talk about it later. You have to go now. Please, give me my key."

Debbie gathered her things and left in a huff. I'd done a rotten thing, sending her home alone so late on her birthday and New Year's Eve, but I knew it had to be done. When God tells you to do something, you'd better obey.

Really, I tried.

25

CHRISTIAN COMPASSION

Consecrating myself to be a better Christian, I devoted myself to life in the spirit and scheduled my Fridays, Saturdays, and Sundays around activities at All Saints Episcopal Church. The sixth week of my spiritual retreat, I met María.

María Miguez sat down next to me at a Friday night worship service. She belonged to the Catholic Church but preferred the more spontaneous flavor that flowed on Fridays at ours. Thirty-two, divorced, with an eight-year-old son, she whispered something to me as we celebrated communion.

After the service, I invited her to continue our conversation over coffee. Her son, Justin, was spending the weekend with his father, and Jonah was with Barbara. "Nice car," she commented as I opened the door for her to my BMW. Nice lady, I thought, as we drove to the local Bob's Big Boy.

María was about five foot four, had black hair cut in a Farrah Fawcett style, and exuded that sultry Mediterranean look that always appealed to me. She was richly attired in a scarlet body-hugging coatdress with scalloped neckline, embellished by a plain, solid gold necklace.

Peopled by money, All Saints had an upper-crust reputation. It was evident that María had class and knew how to spend her money favorably. Over coffee and dessert, I learned her husband was a well-heeled lawyer who had left María for his secretary but provided generous guilt money in alimony and child support.

María had me over for dinner that Sunday night. She lived in a townhouse, richly appointed in leather, cherry wood, and assorted antiques. A part-time dietitian for Fairfax County schools, she cooked up a Spanish meal. Another plus, I thought, assuming that María and Rosie Greene would have something in common to anchor a friendship.

Dinner was leisurely. Afterwards, we retired to the living room where we sat, side by side, on a loveseat and finished the bottle of red wine I'd brought. We didn't run out of things to discuss. I said good-bye with a neat hug and kiss at eleven o'clock, asking if she'd like to come to my place next Saturday for a cookout. I'd have Jonah, and it was her weekend with Justin. The boys were almost the same age, and I wanted them to meet.

Barbara dropped off Jonah at about noon on Saturday, just as María and Justin pulled into my driveway in her silver Mercedes 190E. María smiled tartly and said hello; Barbara held her tongue, giving María the once-over. María didn't hesitate to stare back. Hell may have no fury like a woman scorned, but the eyes of these two smoldered with fiendish contempt over the real victim here—me.

"Make sure he's home by five tomorrow," Barbara demanded as she slammed shut the driver's side door of her Honda.

"Real friendly, isn't she?" María observed condescendingly, closing the front door behind us.

How I loved Christian compassion!

Jonah seemed to like Justin and vice versa, but my son was shy and retiring around women. María was no exception. She tried to get him to talk about his school, friends, and sports, but Jonah answered her questions with one- or two-word sentences and preferred to hide behind me.

"Give him time," María suggested. "It's hard on kids to adjust, to accept new people in their parents' lives. Justin still blames me for his father leaving, and we've had some difficult moments. They're too young to understand why adults make decisions that affect their lives so drastically. It's hard enough for us to cope. Jonah is probably going through the same difficult adjustment as Justin. He misses his family and wants his mother and father to get back together."

María was probably right. I knew that Jonah faulted Barbara for her yelling and tirades, assuming her uncontrolled outbursts were what drove us apart. It's difficult for an only child caught in the middle of parental strife to be without an ally, so Jonah soon began to look to Justin as an older brother.

Four times each week, I drove to María's house for dinner and companionship. We watched TV, played Scrabble, and dissected our marriages.

I'd stretch out on the couch atop María, squirming but fully clothed. The heavy petting was frustrating, but, as Christians, we agreed amorous affection was limited by the church's moral restrictions. Nevertheless, we only were human. Had my foreplay been more aggressive, I'm certain María would have been a willing participant in bringing our ersatz lovemaking to a climax.

* * *

As we approached the third month of seeing each other, a number of things began to change. The novelty had worn off, and María began pushing for a more permanent commitment. She wanted to get married. But I was still married to Barbara, and our separation had become more amicable. Barbara would call me if she needed help around the house—mowing the lawn, fixing a running toilet, or moving some furniture. We talked without animosity and even spent some weekends together going to the movies, taking excursions to amusement parks, or attending school functions with Jonah.

"Are you still praying for me and for us?" she asked me one night.

"Every day," I admitted, curious about what she was getting at.

"I think it's making a difference. I'm beginning to feel a peace about things. Don't misunderstand, Bruce. We've got lots of problems, but I think there may be hope in working them out now."

Standing in the kitchen, I hugged her. Her hand resting on the back of my head, she pulled my face toward hers. Clinging to each other, we kissed with abandon.

There's something anointed about familiarity based on years of shared intimacy. Our techniques had been enhanced by lessons learned from other partners, but the comfortable knowledge of one's spouse is an intangible ingredient that can't be equaled by any number of dating relationships, no matter how intense or passionate. Under the circumstances, the unexpected encounter added an illicit element of excitement to our spontaneous embrace.

"So where do we go from here?" I asked.

"I don't really know," she said, "but we'd better take things slowly."

26

DOUBLE JEOPARDY

Quixotically, I was involved with two women. One was a fiery, jealous Latin who wanted to consummate our relationship within the bonds of holy matrimony. The other was my wife. Both had justifiable claims on me, and neither had my undivided attention. Barbara, of course, knew about María, but María had no idea of my rekindled attraction and attention to Barbara.

Making excuses about being overwhelmed with work, I reduced my visits to María to two weeknights and Saturdays. We saw each other on Sundays, in church. Barbara and I got together on Fridays. At least one night each week, I went over to her place ostensibly to spend time with Jonah and help him with his homework. After I put him to bed, Barbara and I would sit in her living room listening to music and smooching like newlyweds.

We talked, too.

I confessed my shortcomings and remorse for allowing her to feel so neglected. It didn't really matter whether I actually had forsaken her, I agreed. What mattered was that she felt that way. For her part, Barbara asked my forgiveness for treating me so shabbily. She was sorry for having committed adultery, although she still felt justified in her actions. Old hurts and misunderstandings were covered in our conversations, but we never got down to the nitty-gritty of whether—and how—we wanted to try again.

María, meanwhile, suspected something was up. She knew, intuitively, that I was putting her on hold . . . trying to figure out my future and if she was to be included. It was Jonah, finally, who let the cat out of the bag. One weekend when he was with me while I was with María and Justin, Jonah said something at the dinner table about us spending time together at his mother's house. An innocent comment, no doubt. But it added fuel to the fire.

"What's going on?" María confronted me after we'd finished eating. "Please be honest with me. Are you seeing Barbara again?"

"Not exactly," I wavered. "We have been spending time together, but I wouldn't call it seeing each other—not the way you mean."

"Well, how *do* you mean?"

"Things have improved between us, and I'm glad, for Jonah's sake. He's really happy when we do things together as a family. But Barbara hasn't changed much in the things that caused problems between us. She still doesn't eat. She can't or won't budget her money . . . she's in debt up to her ears, running up more than $2,000 in credit card charges. She's not taking care of herself, insisting on doing her schoolwork and laundry and vacuuming until early into the morning, and not getting enough sleep. And," I concluded, "she won't make up her mind about God. She says she believes Jesus is the Messiah, but she won't accept him as Lord. She's adamant about not getting involved with an overbearing church filled with holy rollers who want to tell her how to live her life."

"So what are you going to do?"

"I really don't know."

"Well, you'd better make up your mind. You can't have it both ways. I suggest you think hard and long about what kind of life you want and who's going to be better for you. You're going to have to choose between Barbara and me."

Those were the last words María ever spoke to me.

* * *

As I drove home that evening, a couple of verses from Deuteronomy echoed in my mind: *See, I set before you today life and prosperity, death and destruction . . . Now choose life, so that you and your children may live.*

The choice was made for me the following weekend.

Barbara and I saw each other several times that week. On Friday, she asked if she could come to church with Jonah and me that Sunday. Since María attended the 11:30 service with me after I taught Sunday school at 9:30, I made arrangements for someone to cover my class and accompanied Barbara and Jonah to the earlier service. Wouldn't you know it, María had decided to attend the 9:30 service, too.

I could see tears in her eyes as María, head held high, walked past the pew where we usually sat that now berthed Barbara, Jonah, and me. It was difficult to concentrate on the service. The concluding words, "Go in peace," certainly didn't apply to us. I had to visit the rest room and told Barbara I'd meet her downstairs, under the transept. When I came out, I saw Barbara and María exchanging words in the hallway. María walked past me without saying a word.

"What was that all about?" I asked my wife, nodding toward María.

"Nothing" was all she would say.

Barbara liked All Saints Episcopal Church. She enjoyed the liturgy and felt less conspicuous among the hundreds of parishioners. That was a good start. After church, we went out to lunch. As usual, Barbara had a salad heaped with cottage cheese. I didn't comment. Then we went back to her place and talked seriously about our future. We decided to give our marriage another try.

In short order, we worked out the logistics: Barbara and Jonah would move back in with me. My roommates agreed to switch residences and assume the lease on her townhouse. Barbara would attempt to get her finances in order. She would keep her paycheck from teaching and pay for groceries.

Not having to pay child support any longer, I'd be responsible for the costs of running our household. I'd be allowed to work in my office until dinner; after then, my time would belong to Barbara and Jonah. We also agreed to go for marriage counseling together, albeit with one proviso: Barbara's eating habits wouldn't become a topic of analysis.

Recalling Andrew's advice—Barbara needed to repent for the sin of adultery, she had to seek professional help for her eating disorder, and together, we should participate in marriage counseling to put our house in order—I thought that two out of three weren't that bad.

* * *

Our reconciliation lasted about six months. At first, things seemed to be going relatively well, as we walked on eggshells around each other. Day by day, however, our relationship degenerated as the stresses and strains of unresolved tensions got the better of us.

We started drifting apart, going our separate ways and spending less time together. Barbara had her friends and I had mine. Courteously, she would ask if I'd mind watching Jonah while she went out on a Saturday night. More often than not, I stayed home and brooded. Things just weren't working out.

Finally, we decided to call it quits. Neither of us was really happy, and going through the motions of trying to make our marriage work was becoming more an irritation than a consolation. We were pleasant enough to each other as the days to our final separation neared. Barbara would be moving to Belle and Phil's on a temporary basis while she looked for teaching work in Maryland. I would stay in the house and look for another set of roommates.

Barbara wanted to retain the status quo indefinitely in terms of our marital status. Why, she asked, couldn't we just maintain an ongoing legal separation? I, however, needed to get on with my life and close the book on this long chapter. We sat down together with an attorney and arranged the terms of our divorce, custody and child support, and a property settlement. It would be an uncontested divorce contingent solely on living apart without cohabitating for one year.

* * *

When the day of Barbara's move arrived, Phil drove up in a rented U-Haul truck. Belle wasn't with him—she was watching Jonah—and he refused to look at me. I left the house for the neighborhood swimming pool as Barbara and her father collected the items she was taking. When I returned, dusk already had fallen. It was dark out, yet the street lights illuminated a Honda Prelude parked in front of the house.

"You've got some company," Barbara said, telling me she was ready to leave. "He's waiting in the living room."

"He, who? Who is it?" I asked.

"One of your students."

"A student? What's he doing here?"

"I've got no idea. Ask him yourself," she replied, shutting the door behind her for the last time.

Lounging in my living room, drinking a beer, was Craig McAllister.

"I hope you don't mind my dropping by like this," he began. "I was in the neighborhood and wanted to ask your advice about something. I hoped it would be okay if I came over to talk. Do you mind?"

Did I mind? That his explanation sounded a bit too contrived . . . or that he was there, alone, in my living room?

I admired the gorgeous hunk of man reclining in my favorite chair. Craig was wearing a tank top that left little doubt about his defined assets. He had strong arms with dark ribbons of hair lacing their way up from his wrists to nicely rounded arm muscles. The bottom of his shirt fell about three inches above the top of his Bermuda shorts. A wide thatch of bristly growth covered the exposed area between his T-shirt and shorts. Muscular legs also sprouted thick, curly hair from their feet to the point where they disappeared into his pants. Shiny strands of hair haphazardly fell across his forehead, below which hazel eyes haughtily peered. A cowlick added a lick of slightly sloppy insouciance to his casual aplomb.

Did I mind?

Not in the least. I was thrilled. Barbara and Jonah were gone and, for the first time, Craig and I were together outside the classroom. Inside my house. I excused myself to change out of my swimming trunks, anxious to see what he wanted.

Also dressed in a T-shirt and shorts, I returned with the beer and plopped myself down at the end of the living room sectional sofa. Craig got up from the chair and seated himself in the corner adjacent to me, our knees just inches apart.

"So, how're you doing?" I asked, worried that my trembling knee would knock into his. "Can I get you another beer?"

"Sure, thanks," he said, and I padded into the kitchen.

"I'm doing all right, I guess," he continued, as I returned and handed him the beer. "I just don't know what to do with my life now that college is over. I've got a part-time job selling printing, but I'm living at home with my parents again. It's not what I want."

"Well, what do you want?"

"I'm still not really sure. That's why I wanted to talk with you."

"Why me? How can I help you?"

Was it my imagination, or had Craig's knee made contact with mine? I moved about an inch away. Sure enough, before thirty seconds passed, I again felt an ever so slight brush of the hair on his leg against me.

"Well, I'm sure you know a lot of people in public relations and publishing. Do you know anyone who might have a job opening?"

"Is that what you want to do, Craig, go into PR or communications?"

"I think so."

"You're going to have to be a lot more determined and aggressive than that," I charged, feeling my face become flushed as I realized the double entendre challenge of my words.

"You have to begin by knowing what you want. Remember what the Rolling Stones said? *You can't always get what you want . . . but if you try, sometimes you'll find you get what you need.*"

Craig moved closer and boldly placed his hand on my leg.

"What I want now is to go upstairs with you," he mouthed huskily.

I got up and he followed me to the bedroom. Each waited for the other to make the first move. Craig finally asked if I had any Vaseline. I opened the bottom drawer of the nightstand and handed him the lubricant.

"Get on the bed and lie back," he commanded. "I've wanted to do this for a long time."

When it was over, Craig asked me to promise that what had happened between us wouldn't affect what I thought of him. Right! How could it not?

The next morning, I tried calling him at home to see if he was okay. I needed to hear his voice and reassure myself that our evening together indeed had occurred. I wanted to know when I'd see him again. And I wanted to share an interesting idea with him that I had wrestled with during the night: Craig could rent one of my rooms. He'd be able to get out of his parent's house and move into mine.

His mother said he wasn't home. She took down my number and promised to give him a message to call me. He didn't—not that day, the next, or the day after that. I waited over a month for his call, but it never came.

I felt guilty. I'd given into lust and committed an unpardonable sin, according to what had been preached.

"Please forgive me, God," I prayed. "I'm sorry for disappointing you again. If you forgive me this time, I promise I'll never do it again!"

27

Amanda

People made a point of telling me that Amanda was pretty. It usually was their first comment upon meeting her. "She's so pretty," they'd say; but did they really mean it? It was important to me what other people thought.

I'll admit image always has played an important role in my life and my work. *"We look good when you look better"* was my company's motto; ImageMakers was its name . . . until a number of Christians warned me that the Bible forbids us to make images.

Still, I taught my college public relations classes that one's "identity is the personality you project, the image people perceive," and I endeavored to project a debonair personality, expecting people to perceive me that way. It helped to attract the kind of people with whom I wanted to be associated. Amanda appealed to my image, I thought, at least superficially.

If you'd asked me who she resembled, I suppose I'd say Amanda was a cross between Connie Selleca and Maria Shriver, women I typically found attractive. She stood about five feet, four inches, and had the most angular features I'd ever seen. Her face was all planes: a pointed jaw; jutting chin; and long, linear cheek bones.

Amanda had long, dark hair, which—depending on the effort she took with a dryer to tame it—could either look wantonly messy or shiny and lustrously groomed. Slender and slight, she had beautiful legs, but her breasts were so small that she wore a camisole so you couldn't peek in if she bent down and her blouse separated from her body. She said she was modest.

* * *

We met at All Saints Church about six weeks after Barbara and I separated for the second time. Amanda was visiting for the first time with her sister, Allison, who had joined our congregation several months earlier.

Not knowing that the youngsters whom I taught in Sunday school were mentally—not physically—challenged, Amanda stopped by to drop off her daughter before services.

Juliana was deaf and incredibly bright. My class wasn't appropriate for her, but we chatted a bit, and Amanda gave me her telephone number. I called her that evening. She had a sotto voice, easy to listen to, and we spoke for over an hour. In addition to Juliana, who was seven, she had a four-year-old son, Joshua. The three of them lived with her parents in a Reston townhouse. Amanda had just turned 30, the youngest of the four Fabrezio children.

Her sister Allison was on her second marriage. She had married her high school sweetheart and moved to Boston, where she'd given birth to a daughter and son. When Allison learned that her husband enjoyed dressing up in women's clothing, she bundled the kids up and moved back to her parents' home in Reston. Within three months, she had gotten a job selling jewelry and had become engaged to David, the store manager, who had a pleasant face and a mop of dark, curly hair. Jewish, David had been adopted at birth and agreed to adopt Allison's children, since their biological father was willing to renounce his claim on the children.

As a professed Christian, however, Allison insisted David first accept her beliefs and convert before they married and the adoption could proceed. Wanting to get out from under her parents' roof, she pushed David to hurry his profession of faith. I would learn more about David and Allison over the following months but, in the meantime, was glad to hear of another Jew who believed in Jesus.

Amanda had to cut short our conversation to put her children to bed. Before hanging up, however, I asked if she'd like to go out for dinner.

"I'd like to," she said, but couldn't quite yet, as she still had some things to resolve before she would date or begin a relationship. But I extracted a promise that she'd let me know when she was ready.

It was two months before I saw or heard from her again.

* * *

One Sunday when John, her husband, had the children, Amanda returned to All Saints. Though Juliana wasn't with her this time, she came by my class and sat quietly in the back of the room, observing how I interacted with the youngsters. As we got ready to leave for Children's Chapel, she approached me with a smile, saying I was really quite good with the kids. In an awkward pause that punctuated our dialogue, I sensed she was about to say something else.

"Are you ready to go out yet?" I asked her.

"I think so," she hesitantly agreed.

"What made you change your mind about going out?"

"Several things," she explained. "Watching you work with the Sunday school kids, I was convinced that you really must have a good heart. You impressed me. I decided that it's time for me to move on with my life. I've dated a little during my separation from John, but I wasn't particularly interested in any of the men who pursued me. Besides," she added, "there was something Allison said."

Amanda's sister claimed to have the gift of prophecy. Though we'd never met, Allison saw me sitting in the pews far below where they were seated in the balcony section. She pointed me out to Amanda, said I was 37, and told her sister that I was the man God wanted her to marry.

I shuffled nervously and asked if she believed what Allison said.

"I'm not sure," Amanda replied. "How old are you?"

"Thirty-seven."

The silence between us intruded before I continued.

"Do you want to get married again?" I asked.

"Sure, when I meet the right man. But he would have to be really special, someone who'd want to take care of me and my kids. I'd prefer him to be older, good-looking, about six feet tall, intelligent, and financially responsible. I'm sure I could love and marry someone like that, if he were a Christian. Do you know anyone?"

"We'll see," I offered. "If I think of someone, I'll let you know."

"How about you? What do you want in a woman?"

"The antithesis of my mother. I need someone who can be assertive, but not domineering, accepting instead of demanding, a giver over a taker. Hopefully, she'll be soft and demure, not hard or unyielding, and forgiving rather than always remembering every alleged wrong. In short, I want a saint, not a martyr."

"Hmmm" was her only response.

Despite differences in our backgrounds, our mothers evidently were quite similar: bossy, uncompromising, selfish, spiteful, intimidating, take-charge heads of their households.

We had covered a lot of ground in our two telephone conversations, and I was eager to continue the getting-to-know-you process over dinner, so I made a date to take her out for dinner that Friday after John came to pick up the kids.

* * *

As I drove through Reston and turned onto her street, I noticed that Amanda lived only a few blocks from my friend Angela Fletcher who, weeks earlier, had left her job as director of communications at a nearby non-profit organization to become my business partner.

I parked in Amanda's driveway and knocked on the door. Her mother, Vivian, opened it. Saying her daughter would be right down, she invited me into the living room and began a good-natured conversation.

"She doesn't seem all that bad," I told Amanda, as I opened the passenger's side door to my car and helped her get in.

"You obviously made a good impression. Wait till you get to know her better. She's one of the most opinionated and vocal people you'll ever meet." Changing the subject, Amanda told me that my burgundy BMW 325i was her favorite make, model, and color of car. Until he was fired, John had worked for three months as a salesman at a BMW dealership.

Our earlier phone conversation had compared the complexities of our families and mothers. Now, over dinner, we talked about the trials and tribulations we experienced with our respective spouses.

Amanda had been separated from John for over eighteen months. He was a real bastard who'd abused her physically, emotionally, and financially. A Bible-waving bigot, John spouted scriptures which suited his purposes, but he had been "disfellowshipped" from three churches because of his lying spirit and malicious deeds.

In retaliation, John renounced these congregations as "being of the devil," obtained a mail-order ordination, and began his own fellowship with the half-dozen or so people who, for whatever reason, still believed in him.

John didn't work; he fancied himself an inventor of gadgets and conned a number of people (including Amanda's parents, relatives, and neighbors) into financing his schemes. When the money ran out after buying clothing, cars, and computers, John turned to preying and wielding his charms on little old ladies whom he had befriended. They would loan him money and credit cards of which he took carte blanche advantage. Sooner or later, they realized how much they had been victimized by him and wrote John off, tearfully reporting his transgressions to Amanda.

Amanda, of course, had enough of her own problems with John. He never paid their bills, had amassed quite substantial debts, and Amanda no longer was able to justify or make excuses for him. She was tired of getting phone calls warning that their phone and utilities would be disconnected, the car repossessed, or that they were dangerously close to being evicted from their apartment.

Worse, John had threatened her repeatedly, and she literally was scared to death of him. He had hit her and shoved her around while she was pregnant with Juliana, and Amanda suspected that could be why their daughter was born deaf. Later, John hid Amanda's birth control pills, and she soon became pregnant with Joshua. Their divorce dragged on because John sought custody of the children. In the meantime, he was supposed to pay Amanda $225 each month in child support for both children . . . which he hardly ever did, and certainly never on time.

Amanda's attorney told her he could have John thrown in jail, but she was afraid that would just add insult to injury as he attempted to alienate the children.

"See what your mother did to me," he'd cry. "She had me put in jail."

The children were strangely attached to their father and faulted Amanda for leaving him. That John was wrong and a judge rightfully had incarcerated him to atone for his own deeds didn't matter. This would be another weapon for John to use in undermining any affection between the children and their mother.

The straw that broke the proverbial camel's back was John's cheating, with women as well as with finances. Amanda discovered a poem in his pocket written by a "friend" living downstairs, with whom John clearly had spent the night.

When John left the next morning, Amanda drove the kids and her few possessions over to her parents' house.

"Heard enough?" she paused and asked.

"What made you marry him in the first place?"

"The church. They insisted it was God's will for me to marry John, and had me convinced that he could be redeemed. John was my 'mission field,' they said. I tried to back out of the marriage about a week before the wedding, but it was too late. I'd made my bed and I had to lie on it."

"But didn't you tell them about the awful stuff John did to you?"

"Of course. It didn't matter, though. Everyone believed that John had these special gifts, which just needed to be nurtured. 'Hang in there,' they told me. 'He'll change.' We were married for five years, but he never changed; he only got worse. And later, I found out that things I had shared in confidence with the church were being spread around the congregation. Everyone knew my business, and I couldn't stand it. When I left John, I left that church. No matter how bad the circumstances, they believe that marriage is forever. After all, 'God hates divorce.' As far as they're concerned, I'm a bigger sinner for leaving John than he is, no matter what he's done or how much we've suffered."

I thanked God I no longer was part of such a demoralizing church. Although All Saints was a spirit-filled, mainline denomination, John held that Episcopalians were only one step removed from the Roman Catholic church, which he called the Babylonian harlot—the same words he used to denounce Amanda to her young, impressionable children. In God's eyes, John swore, he and Amanda would always be married, and any dating she did with other men ultimately would bring condemnation and eternal damnation on her soul.

Leaving Amanda at her parents' front door, she thanked me for an enjoyable evening. We lingered and kissed, and I asked if I would see her again on Sunday at church. She nodded.

* * *

I thought about Amanda all day Saturday and was delighted to see her the next day—with Juliana and Joshua. We sat together during the service and, afterward, went out for lunch. Amanda introduced me to her sister, Allison, who had driven everyone to church that morning. I invited Allison and her children, Scott and Sophie, to accompany us, but she demurred for another occasion, saying we should have some time alone now. Promising to return them to Reston, I gave Allison a good-natured hug.

Lunch was a harried experience, with Juliana constantly interrupting and Joshua begging for attention. It was understandable, I thought: Although Juliana was quite proficient at reading lips, unless she looked directly at you, she was unaware that other people were talking. Joshua obviously had suffered emotionally from the tug-of-war between his estranged parents. Juliana, however, had been indoctrinated by her father and was wary around me. Nonetheless, Joshua reveled in the company of his mother's new friend and was thrilled to let me lift him onto my shoulders as we exited the restaurant and walked through the parking lot.

I took them to Chuck E Cheese, where I bought ten dollars worth of tokens and let the kids enjoy the amusements. Amanda and I sat at a table holding hands and talking as the children were diverted by the arcade's many novelties. Their father didn't allow them to watch television, play video games, or indulge in such "satanic" attractions, so they took full advantage of the cornucopia's delights.

We got back to Reston at six o'clock, and Amanda's folks invited me to stay for dinner. Allison and her kids came over. The adults ate in the dining room, while children were assigned to the kitchen.

About ten thirty, I thanked Vivian for her hospitality, said my goodbyes, and told everyone I looked forward to seeing them again soon. Amanda accompanied me outside, pressing herself against me at the door of my car and running her fingers through my hair.

"I really had a nice time today," she sighed. "Thanks for giving me some hope again." We kissed for a while and I slipped my hand inside her blouse, rubbing the small of her back. She mewed a sound of contentment, something between a moo and a moan.

28

A Big Mistake?

Amanda and I took turns calling each other every night, talking for over an hour. During the first month of our relationship, we saw each other Sundays at church and either Friday or Saturday evenings. We were on the same schedule with our kids—weekends when John had Juliana and Joshua and Barbara had Jonah. And since I usually picked Jonah up on Saturday mornings, my Friday nights were still free. Amanda's parents or sisters volunteered to watch her children on Fridays when she had the kids, so we could have more time alone together.

We ate out a lot. Amanda could put away a heavy meal without putting on a pound, enabling us to enjoy cuisine ranging from fast food to fancier French, Greek, Chinese, and Italian fare.

Naturally, Amanda was curious about what went wrong with my marriage to Barbara. We dwelled on her eating habits, although it was obvious that *that* wouldn't be a problem between Amanda and me. I told her about Barbara's compulsive spending and her inability to live within a budget. After her experience with John, Amanda was more concerned about avoiding bill collectors by saving money than spending it.

We discussed deception. Having been jilted by John for their downstairs neighbor, the last thing Amanda could imagine was cheating on one's spouse.

I mentioned Barbara's flirtation with liberated ladies who liked to step out without their husbands. This was something Amanda simply couldn't fathom.

Although she had an associate's degree in interior decorating, Amanda had no career designs. Necessity required her to work in the public school system as an interpreter for the deaf, and while she was willing to contribute to household finances, she looked forward to a time when her principal avocation would be taking care of her family and being a homemaker. She reiterated that her parents had raised her to believe that women, though strong and capable, should be taken care of by their men.

* * *

It wasn't long before I began taking care of Amanda—physically as well as financially.

Although sometimes I faked it, my inability to have an orgasm didn't deter us from seeking sexual gratification.

Still married to others, we knew our behavior was considered sinful, but I justified it as the lesser of two evils. Convincing myself it was a gift from God to help me avoid other, more reprobate outlets, I rationalized that for me, our sexual conduct was therapeutic.

* * *

By our third month of dating, the decision to marry seemed to be made. I certainly didn't propose and she never asked; we just took it for granted that that was where our relationship was headed. Before either of us was divorced from our respective spouses, we were engaged, and Amanda was wearing a diamond ring we had picked out at the jewelry store where Allison worked.

It was now time to introduce Amanda to my parents.

We flew down to Florida and stayed in their house. I was braced for a confrontation over our sleeping arrangements, but I was glad that my folks just assumed we would share a room. Being able to perform in the room next to my parents seemed to confirm a Freudian suspicion that, if I could do it there and then, I would be able to successfully conquer any sexual handicap.

Any more confirmation I might have needed that Amanda and I were supposed to wed came during a short visit to Lori Kellogg, Jonah's godmother and my close friend from the adoption agency.

Lori was taken by Amanda's love for children and impressed by her hearty appetite. When we told her that we planned to marry in another three months, Lori asked us the exact date.

"Sunday, December 13," I told her.

"You're kidding!" she said, more an exclamation than a question.

"No," I replied, asking her why.

"Because that's my twins' birthday."

Lori had adopted siblings from Korea, naming them Amanda and Elizabeth. Amanda's middle name was Elizabeth. We would be getting married on the birthday of a close friend's daughters who, amazingly, shared the same names of my wife-to-be.

It must be an omen, enthused Lori. *Bashert*—meant to be—insisted my Jewish friends who spoke some Yiddish.

Amanda and I flew back to Northern Virginia, where everyone at All Saints Church was supportive of our decision to marry. We made an appointment with the rector to discuss our wedding plans and learned that, before the church would consent to marry us, we would have to participate in a six-week series of marriage counseling sessions.

Moreover, since neither of us was divorced yet, and the Episcopal Church requires at least two years between a divorce and new marriage, the bishop would have to grant us a special "dispensation."

Since my friendship with Andrew augured a potential conflict of interest, the rector had appointed another priest to work with us.

"Don't worry," advised Rev. George Singleton, our counselor. "The bishop usually respects my recommendation. If I think you're eligible and ready to marry, he'll grant the dispensation without delay."

Every Tuesday afternoon, we met for an hour with Reverend George, who fancied himself an armchair psychologist. We talked about our upbringing, the roles we had played in our respective families, the problems we'd encountered in our previous marriages, and how we would be able to draw upon those experiences to avoid similar disasters once we were wed. George reviewed the obligations incumbent upon a Christian marriage and probed our commitment to the faith . . . as well as to each other.

At our last meeting, George flashed a smile and held out a document he had just received from the diocesan office. Based upon his recommendation, the bishop had agreed to the dispensation that would allow us to be married in the church on the date we had planned. But first, George had one last question to ask.

"Bruce, would you be willing to adopt Amanda's children?"

"Under the right circumstances, I guess. But John would never give up his parental rights." I looked to Amanda for confirmation.

"That's right," she agreed. "He would never, ever, allow Bruce to be their father."

"That's not what I asked," George interjected. "Would you be *willing*, Bruce, to assume legal responsibility for them?"

Amanda's fingers tightened around my hand as I considered the implications of what George was asking. I hadn't really spent that much time with Juliana and Joshua. We hadn't lived together, as Barbara and I did before we married. I didn't really know them or what would be demanded of me.

Words stumbled out of my mouth: "I guess so . . . sure."

I wondered whether I would have cause to regret those words.

* * *

Our counseling completed, Amanda and I busied ourselves with the final plans for our wedding less than a month away. The ceremony itself would take place in the small chapel next to All Saints' current building.

George and Andrew would co-celebrate the union. Since we never had discussed having children—Jonah, Juliana and Joshua seemed plenty for me to handle, and Amanda didn't know if she wanted more children—we requested that the words about being blessed with children be deleted from our vows.

Due to my mother's kidney problems, neither she nor my father could attend. My brother and sisters wouldn't be coming up from Florida, either, although Lori Kellogg—God bless her!—would fly in and out for the day. Tom Greene agreed to be my best man.

An hour after the service, a reception would be held at my home.

Amanda had taken charge of the decorations and ordered food from a local caterer. A musician we both liked from All Saints' praise band would provide piano music on the baby grand in my living room.

Following the service and reception, our wedding night would be spent in the Hyatt Regency at Dulles Airport, where we reserved the bridal suite. We would leave early the next morning for our honeymoon in Cancún, Mexico.

* * *

A week before the ceremony, Amanda and I began making daily treks between Manassas and Reston to bring her belongings to their new home—pots and pans; clothing; toys; linens; files and papers; assorted appliances, furnishings, and bric-a-brac. I had never seen such a mess cluttering my basement. Where would it all go? How would everything fit? Amanda promised to have her things all assorted, organized, and neatly stored when we returned from our honeymoon.

On Saturday, December 13, I arose early; I hadn't really slept much during the night. Meticulously, I showered, shaved, and dressed in the new navy blue pinstripe suit I'd bought myself for the occasion. I looked at the clock. It was eleven am, an hour before the service scheduled to change my life would begin. The church was only a half hour away, but I decided to leave a little early.

Driving down Centreville Road, I turned right onto Lee Highway. Suddenly, I was seized by one of the worst panic attacks I had ever experienced. Fearing I might lose control and consciousness, I gripped the steering wheel hard and turned into the parking lot of a shopping center where I popped a couple of Xanax which I always carried for emergencies. Then I prayed, as I'd never done before.

Was the devil attempting to thwart my future security and happiness? Or was a greater power warning me about making a major mistake?

29

Niggling Doubts, Nagging Insecurities

Marital discord began on our honeymoon. Amanda and I consummated our marriage the way we had consumed our dating relationship—with sex. We coupled before getting out of bed in the morning, after we returned to our hotel room in the afternoon, and again, when we went to sleep at night. By the third day of our entwined life, I was spent.

I craved privacy and space, but the more I pulled away, the more Amanda crowded me. She couldn't comprehend why I felt so suffocated from her constant amorous attention.

In all honesty, neither did I.

Amanda seemed good-natured, inventive, and compassionate. She doted on me and dwelled on my every word. Any man would be thrilled to have such a lovely wife who placed a premium on his happiness. But I felt trapped . . . snared by a familiar bloodsucker draining my lifeline and equanimity.

Following three days and nights of performing husbandly duties, I awkwardly turned the other way and gently nudged Amanda away.

It didn't help matters that I found myself attracted to Julio Hernandez, a local artist whose works were displayed in the lobby of the Cancún Sheraton Hotel. Women would leave messages for Julio telling him how handsome and sexy they found him, inviting him to visit their rooms when their husbands were away. I, however, suspected there was more to Julio's roving than met the eye.

He made a point of befriending me, of putting his arm around my shoulder as we strolled across the hotel grounds. Something in his smile, glance, or touching camaraderie convinced me that Julio's blatant sexuality could swing either way.

Amanda evidently didn't notice my flirtation with Julio; more concerned was she about his girlfriend, Rachel. Beautiful and free-spirited, she paraded around with a scant scarf draped across an ample bosom that left little to the visiting voyeur's imagination. It was my first hint of the jealous anguish that, over the next few years, would chip away at our marriage.

Giving credit where it was due, jealousy was one problem that never troubled Barbara and me. The word wasn't in our vocabulary. Each of us was flirtatious, but we dismissed our playful teasing as innocent fun.

Amanda, however, had quite a different view: No matter how innocent, she believed flirting was totally inappropriate when you were married—whether on the home front or the playing field. Her rule held especially true for Christians.

The Bible is loaded with verses that supported Amanda's concerns:

"But since there is so much immorality, each man should have his own wife, and each woman her own husband. The husband should fulfill his marital duty to his wife, and likewise the wife to her husband. The wife's body does not belong to her alone but also to her husband. In the same way, the husband's body does not belong to him alone but also to his wife," states I Corinthians.

Amanda took these Scriptures literally and used them, indignantly, to support her own convictions. She was jealous of her sister, who she claimed was guilty of meddling in her marriage to John. According to Amanda, Allison had betrayed her, delighting in demeaning and trying to make Amanda believe that, everything else being equal, John would have preferred her elder sister.

My professional affiliation with Angela Fletcher was also a bone of contention between us. Angela and I had become good friends as well as business partners. We spent our days working together and would go out to lunch from time to time. Although I invited Amanda to join us—her job as interpreter for the deaf was at a school just about fifteen minutes from my office—she refused. But that didn't stop her from harping on how spurious it was for Angela and me to share so many interests and common concerns.

While she was jealous of any woman who showed even the slightest interest in me, Amanda was especially annoyed about my relationship with Barbara. Since our divorce, we had managed to put aside most of our past hurts and differences and were actually on rather friendly terms.

I no longer really cared *for* Barbara; but I would always care *about* her.

Barbara would call to tell me about a mutual acquaintance she'd run across, a new movie she'd seen that she thought I would like, a book which might interest me. She'd ask if I'd heard the latest song from a musician we both enjoyed or relate a dream in which my family was involved. And, naturally, we'd talk about Jonah.

Amanda believed it totally inappropriate for Barbara and me to have such discussions; as far as she was concerned, our dealings should be limited to two-minute conversations about Jonah: when I would pick him up on my weekends and the best time for her to come and retrieve him.

* * *

The jealousy conflict ultimately came to a head with Rosie Greene, Tom's wife and my dear friend. Amanda really resented Rosie and was certain that, given the opportunity, Rosie would dump her husband and take off for parts unknown with me and her two young children in tow.

The idea was ridiculous, but so was Amanda's possessiveness.

She couldn't fathom how I could have separate friendships with Tom, Tom and Rosie, and Rosie. Tom was my best friend and, together, he and his wife would socialize with Amanda and me. But I had known Rosie independently of Tom and refereed many a marital crisis between them.

One day, Rosie called to ask my opinion about some advertising and marketing materials she was preparing for her nutrition practice. We were on the telephone over an hour discussing ways to improve and refine her presentation. Throughout the last thirty minutes of our conversation, Amanda stood in the doorway of my office, hands on her hips and a belligerent scowl making her defiant jaw line even stronger.

"What did she want now?" Amanda demanded when I hung up.

"She needed some business advice," I replied, determined to put an end to this silliness.

"Couldn't she call someone else for a change? Why does she always have to speak with you?"

"Because we're friends. She respects my advice . . . and I care."

"Well you shouldn't."

"I shouldn't what?"

"Care. You have no right to care about her. She's not your wife. I am. Why can't her own husband help her?"

"Tom's an attorney, not a wordsmith. And that's beside the point," I spat, gritting my teeth. The strain in my voice was reaching a feverish pitch.

"Don't ever, *ever* tell me who I can and can't care about. My life may revolve around you, but you're not my entire universe. I've just about had it with these stupid, petty jealousies. I'm warning you—they'd better stop. I will not put up with you standing here, eavesdropping on my conversations and interfering with my friendships."

"Is that so?" she challenged, standing her ground by tapping her foot and pointing a finger at me.

"Yes, that's so. I'm not going to deal with this nonsense any longer."

"Or what?"

"I'll leave."

The words stunned me. Amanda's niggling doubts and nagging insecurities really annoyed me, but I didn't expect to hear myself issue such an ultimatum.

"I see," she hissed, slamming the door behind her as she stormed out of my room with tears streaming down her cheeks.

Amanda relished a good fight. I hated it. When Amanda wanted to argue, we would end up in a battle. But, in all honesty, that didn't occur until later . . . when our marriage was almost over.

*   *   *

I had no idea what I was in store when Amanda and her kids moved in. Under the best of circumstances, sharing is difficult for me. I know that the marriage vows state "for better and worse, for richer or poorer, in sickness and health . . . my troth I thee pledge."

Making it so, however, was much easier said than done.

Barbara's inability to live within a set budget and her spendthrift habits had brought us to the brink of bankruptcy. Dividing what little remained of our assets in the property settlement of our divorce agreement left me dangerously close to economic insolvency. Not only was I required to come up with the cash to buy Barbara out of the home we'd purchased, I now had to pay her monthly child support payments for Jonah.

I was financially strapped and swore that, once on my feet again, I'd never allow myself to get into a situation that would compromise my ability to survive. In any event, I believed a second marriage was quite different from the first. Especially financially.

Amanda and I maintained separate checking accounts. Although she expected to be taken care of now by me—and it really bothered me that she had referred to me as "good husband material" rather than saying I would make a good husband—we agreed upon an equitable division of our financial responsibilities: John's meager child support payments and Amanda's interpreting income would be used to purchase our family groceries and pay for her children's unique needs. My contribution would cover the rest of our living expenses.

Unfortunately, John hardly ever met the monthly obligations to his children. What did we expect of him? He wasn't working, so more often than not, even his minimum child support payments weren't made. Amanda tried to stretch her limited income to compensate for the shortfall. But private school tuition for Joshua and paying down her outstanding credit card charges, as well as the substantial costs associated with Julianna's disability and putting food on our table, far exceeded her limited earnings.

Unbeknown to me, she had begun to bounce checks and borrow money from her parents so she wouldn't have to admit her sloppy bookkeeping to me.

Amanda had applied for new credit cards that she used to make many purchases. Until she told me about them, I was unaware of these additional debts. Nonetheless, Amanda believed it was my place as her husband to pay off these charges, even if they were for Joshua's tuition at the Christian school about which she never consulted me.

I disagreed.

I wanted to have John arrested and thrown in jail.

Earlier, I had offered to underwrite Amanda's tuition to attend para-legal school and begin a more lucrative career. Now I was happy to pay an attorney to see that John was punished for abrogating his responsibilities. Allowing him to get away with such contemptible behavior wasn't fair—to Amanda, her children, or to me.

She wouldn't accede to my wishes and rejected both offers offhand. Amanda was petrified of John. She feared his physical retribution and was certain John would take advantage of her actions to prejudice the children.

"See what your mother did to me now," he would say. "She had me put in prison."

That a judge, not Amanda, imposed the sentence wouldn't matter, nor would the children accept that John was indeed guilty of committing a crime. He had a way of getting away with murder.

Our financial situation further deteriorated when Amanda learned her earnings from interpreting would be garnished by the Internal Revenue Service.

John had filed compromised tax returns when he and Amanda were married. The IRS tried to collect its due, but John wasn't working and had no known means of income. He was more than happy, however, to inform the collection agents that his former wife was employed now by Fairfax County Public Schools. Since their tax returns had been signed by both John and Amanda, they were jointly and severally responsible for meeting all obligations. Out of her paltry $200 take-home pay each week, $50 would now be deducted from each check and sent to the Internal Revenue Service.

We made an appointment to talk with a counselor at our local IRS office, but learned that nothing could be done. John and Amanda owed Uncle Sam the money, and she had to repay it since he couldn't . . . or wouldn't.

The counselor's best advice was directed at me. The government could attach anything Amanda and I jointly owned, so don't put anything jointly in both our names, he warned. Especially the house. In buying Barbara out, the house was in my name as *homme seul,* and I never made any effort to change it to reflect my new marital status. Now I had an officially-sanctioned reason to keep it mine alone.

Naturally, this perturbed Amanda. But what could she say? A representative of the Internal Revenue Service had made this suggestion, and it bore the government's official stamp of approval.

"Everyone must submit himself to the governing authorities, for there is no authority except that which God has established," I reminded Amanda, this time acknowledging Romans 13.

30

TURMOIL AND UPHEAVAL

The house became a major source of contention between us.

Amanda had moved in lock, stock, and barrel with two truckloads of keepsakes. Where she had stored all this stuff in her parents' townhouse, I'll never know, but none of it ever got put away.

An analyst once concluded that I needed to control my external environment because I suffered such internal strife and chaos. Everything had to appear just right, to be properly positioned, and neatly in place. That was impossible with Amanda and her kids living in the house.

It seemed to make sense to give Julianna Jonah's room. Without consulting him, Jonah was moved to the second and larger bedroom, which he now shared with Joshua. Slowly but surely, Joshua's things crowded my son's. Until later, when it was too late, I had never realized how much Jonah resented this intrusion on his father, family, and turf.

Julianna was a slob who had inherited her father's selfish disposition. Her room was always a mess. She'd whine and complain about not having enough space, so we allowed her to move into the downstairs guest room. As she demanded even more privacy and range to roam, we permitted her to move into the finished basement.

SQUARE PEG IN A ROUND HOLE

The house was in a constant state of upheaval and turmoil. And Amanda, more than her children, was the worst culprit.

Amanda made little messes . . . "piles" we called them. Her papers would pile up all over the place, never put away. She used every pot and pan in the kitchen to cook and would leave dirty dishes overnight in the sink instead of rinsing them off and stacking them neatly in the dishwasher. I got up before she did in the morning, so making the bed was her responsibility. Time and again, I'd come home to disheveled sheets, unkempt pillows, and bunched up blankets.

The laundry was a major and continuing source of aggravation. Four baskets sat at the bottom of our linen closet, their contents divided between darks, lights, permanent press, and towels. Rather than taking an entire basket, Amanda would grab a bunch from each basket and throw it into the washing machine and dryer, mixing everything together. Before things were dry, she'd remove the damp laundry and leave it in a pile on the floor while beginning another load. Her intentions were good, but for one reason or another (which usually had to do with the children's incessant demands), she never got around to drying, folding, and putting everything away. The wet wash naturally attracted mildew, which pissed me off.

Instead of getting into another heated argument, I bought myself a laundry basket and set it in my closet, into which I placed my dirty clothes. From then on, I did my own laundry.

When Amanda discovered my little indiscretion, it set off a week of hurtful exchanges. I was simply trying to avoid any confrontation and make her life easier by washing my clothes the way I wanted them done. But, for Amanda, this was one of two crises that signaled our marriage had begun to spiral its downward dive.

* * *

The other incident occurred at Angela's house, when we were invited to dine with "Eaters Anonymous," a group of elderly friends who met monthly for a meal and earnest debate. While someone else determined and assigned the food to be prepared, the host or hostess was responsible for coming up with a theme for the evening's discourse.

Weary of discussing Jewish issues and U.S. support of Israel (the eaters were anonymous except for their religious persuasions), Angela proposed that our topic that evening deal with the reasons romance always seemed to go out of marriages.

Except for Angela, Amanda and me, the group's median age hovered around 75 . . . and most had been married for about 50 years.

"Romance, *shmomance,*" they said. Why was that so important to Angela? A successful marriage, they maintained, was achieved by accepting your spouse and then learning to look the other way.

Angela disagreed and began the discussion with an example from her own marriage. "Why doesn't Tom take more care and pride in his dressing habits," she asked, "even if we're only at home together? Shouldn't he be concerned about making a good impression on me? Look at him," she pointed disdainfully. "He insists on wearing old tattered clothes even though I've bought him some nice new shirts and slacks."

"I know what you mean," I offered, catching her drift as the rest of the group nodded off in their chairs. "It's different when you're dating and don't see each other all of the time. We want to make our best impressions, primping and trying to look our best. After marriage, we tend to get lazy. We don't pay enough attention to how we look. Amanda always wears this old housecoat and doesn't take the time anymore to fix her hair or face. When you see someone first thing every morning without any makeup . . ."

Amanda shot me daggers, while Angela bit her lip to stifle a smile. Though she was well aware of the predicament I had gotten myself into, Angela had little sympathy for my wife, who, for some reason, deliberately had gone out of her way to let Angela know that she'd seen dog hair in her butter dish. Talk about how not to win friends and influence people—particularly when they're not especially fond of each other to begin with!

Berating me for insulting her in front of a bunch of strangers, Amanda refused to say another word to me all week. If it weren't for the kids, who'd be with us the next weekend, I'm certain my penance would have dragged on even longer.

* * *

Amanda and I had tried to structure visitations around our own convenience. One weekend, we had all the children together; the next, we had none of them. The arrangement gave us time alone every other weekend, but our children never had an opportunity to be with us independently and treated uniquely. Except for what Barbara later told me, I would never have known that Jonah felt lost and unhappy.

Barbara was Jonah's primary caretaker, a strong mother who made it difficult for him to accept Amanda. And Amanda didn't relish being cast in the role of wicked stepmother.

Maybe I was too lax, allowing Jonah to get away with stuff he wouldn't under ordinary circumstances. But I saw him only twice each month, so a little latitude, I believed, was in order. Amanda assumed the role of disciplinarian, chastising Jonah—along with Joshua and Juliana—for any misbehavior.

My son resented her; Amanda's children refused to acknowledge me.

I wasn't their father, John insisted, making a point of telling Juliana and Joshua that they didn't have to heed my instructions. I'll never forget how he had given Juliana his 10 X 14 framed photograph, urging her to display it in her room. As if it wasn't bad enough that his children were encouraged to undermine my authority, I now had to live with a large portrait of John hanging in my house!

In other ways, too, John's presence cast a long shadow over the gathering storm of our marriage. John was flighty and undependable. Loosely translated, that meant the weekends alone that Amanda and I truly cherished almost never materialized.

"Something came up. It just couldn't be helped," he would shrug when he didn't call or show up for the kids on weekends we'd made plans. Amanda refused to talk to him directly, so it fell on me to serve as mediator. We heard about John's underhanded schemes and shenanigans, as his latest victims sought refuge around our kitchen table to tell us their tales of woe.

Amanda and I disagreed about how to handle the children.

I felt she was too hard on Juliana and not strict enough with Joshua. Amanda believed I favored Juliana and didn't understand Joshua. She sensed that I avoided family pursuits and didn't spend quality time with the children. In that regard, Amanda was right. Except for our scheduled "family outings" when Jonah was with us, I kept my distance.

I preferred to eat by myself, away from the bickering and food fights each night at the dinner table. Later I'd retreat to the privacy of my office, hoping to hide from the children's constant demands. I knew I was fleeing from parental responsibilities, so I made good-faith efforts to compensate for my shortcomings. I would help Joshua with his homework, take Juliana to the gym, be sure to tuck the children in bed, and wish them good night.

But it never came naturally and always required effort.

31

POSTPONING THE INEVITABLE

For my fortieth birthday, Amanda planned a surprise party, arranging for entertainment—dance instructors who would teach us to jitterbug, tango, and cha-cha—and inviting many of my friends.

Before then, we devised an ingenious idea to make our "extended" family more integrated and compatible. John and Barbara both shared eccentric eating habits and, in many other ways, seemed to be sort of well matched. So, for the family's sake, we invited them over together for dinner. What a disaster that was! Barbara found John to be a belligerent ne'er-do-well, and he thought of her as the most eerie, highest-maintenance infidel he'd ever had the misfortune to meet.

We had better luck with another attempt at matchmaking. From the moment I met him, I believed that Amanda's brother-in-law, David, and Barbara would be perfect for each other.

"Don't misunderstand," I told Amanda. "I sincerely hope nothing bad happens between Allison and David. But if anything ever should, I think he and Barbara would really like each other."

Amanda agreed. Believe it or not, so did her sister.

Allison was returning to school to major in drama, shedding her domestic diva and her family along the way.

"David's a nice guy," she acknowledged, "but he's boring. He's become more of a friend than a lover and, at this point in my life, I want someone who's supportive of my acting career. I need the freedom to come and go when I want. I just can't be married to him anymore."

This came from a crusading Christian who saw no contradiction between her religious convictions and personal pilgrimage.

It was Allison who first suggested that we try fixing David up with Barbara. And it was Allison who called my ex-wife to promote David's virtues. Wouldn't you know it, they really hit it off together! Barbara and David dated about six months. It was an interesting, albeit awkward, situation for everyone involved. Yet we saw several redeeming, human-interest virtues in the relationship and thought it would be amusing to share our extraordinary experience with others.

I contacted the producers of the *Oprah* show, with whom I had worked before to arrange publicity for one of my clients. "Ex-changing spouses," I proposed as a potential program segment, hopefully hooking them with a loaded question: What happens when husbands and wives serve as matchmakers for their former spouses? The clincher, I wrote, was my son's rather innocent question. Jonah wanted to know how many mothers he would have if Barbara did marry David.

Jonah knew he had a birth mother in El Salvador; Barbara was the only real mother he knew; and, through my second marriage, Amanda had become his stepmother. Since David was the stepfather to Allison's two kids, would Allison also become his stepmother now?

Wouldn't you know it, the producers bit. They loved the concept! It had all the *sturm und drang* of a real-life soap opera—drama, humor, conflict, and machinations. Amazingly, they told us we weren't alone; their researchers had been able to locate other couples in related relationships who were willing to appear along with us on the show.

I was the one who received the producers' call saying they wanted to schedule us for the show. Nonetheless, first they needed to corroborate the information I had already supplied.

We went over my letter, point by point, verifying that everything I'd told them was true. Next, they wanted telephone numbers for Barbara, David, and Allison, as well as Amanda's at work.

To ensure the validity of my statements, it was necessary to contact each of the involved parties and get their input on the issue. Even more important, however, in scheduling the show was to confirm that all of the principal players were available and would be willing to appear. Without everyone on stage together, the segment would lose much of its pathos.

Following my conversation with the show's producers, Amanda, Barbara, and David each were called. All agreed that what I had told them was true, and we all volunteered to do the show. Allison's take on the matter, however, created some problems. As an aspiring actress, she was thrilled with the opportunity to tell her story on national television. Still, she insisted on couching it as a Christian witness, preaching the good news about how Jesus loves sinners and is able to redeem even seemingly absurd relationships.

Oprah wouldn't hear of it. Her show wasn't the time or the place for this kind of proselytizing. Unable to persuade Allison to play by the rules, we had to withdraw from participating on the show and wait to be contacted when another "panel of experts" could be scheduled.

By the time we had heard from the producers again, it was already too late. Barbara and David had split up, and Amanda and I were separated.

* * *

One big problem in our marriage was different attitudes about and expectations of a second marriage.

There was no difference between a first and the second, Amanda believed. Marriage was marriage, she said, and she expected me to be her knight in shining armor. From my point of view, however, a second marriage brought echoes of the past along with it. John shouldn't neglect his responsibilities to his children, and Amanda's responsibility was to ensure he lived up to his obligations. As for Barbara, she would always be a part of my life whether Amanda liked it or not.

I talked about going for counseling, but Amanda wouldn't hear of it. She'd been through it before, with John, at their church. The upshot was that everyone knew her business, and even though she had been repeatedly wronged, the church ministers always forgave John and advised her to do likewise. Seeing a "secular" counselor was out of the question, too, since he (or she) wouldn't understand the special covenant between a Christian couple.

Taking the Scarlett O'Hara "I'll think about it tomorrow" approach wasn't working anymore; after all, tomorrow only brought another day of bellicosity. I was becoming more inconsolable and depressed, even despondent, over the situation and didn't know what to do any longer.

Fiddle-dee-dee, what were my options?

Doubling my daily dose of Xanax, perhaps, would help to relieve the anxiety, enabling me to continue repressing my feelings and frustrations. But I couldn't deny them. I could beg (force?) Amanda to go for counseling with me, to discuss our difficulties, and attempt to resolve them. Counseling would buy us some time, but would it only postpone the inevitable? Of course, we could split up and put an end to a marriage probably mistaken right from the start. Or, I could insist on a trial separation that would give me some time and space to put my life into perspective.

Fortunately, a business-oriented separation was soon on the calendar.

32

CRITICAL CROSSROADS

Each year I handled publicity and public relations for one of my major accounts, a trade association representing a large segment of the printing industry, at its annual convention and trade show. I would be in Los Angeles for ten days, away from Amanda and our mounting marital problems.

In some cities, attracting positive publicity isn't all that difficult: You develop an interesting angle, prepare appropriate press materials, contact the media to arrange convenient times for making courtesy calls, spend a few minutes with them pitching your story. You remind your contacts about the "opportunity" by contacting them again the morning the event is to happen. Then, you sit back and wait, hoping and praying they'll show up . . . that no "hard" news like murders, robberies, fires, or other disasters pre-empts the time that otherwise may be allotted to your story.

Los Angeles is different. Selling a story that's not somehow related to Hollywood is difficult in the city of angels.

Elsewhere, publicists can gain access to the places where the media work: newspaper buildings, radio stations, television broadcasting facilities. In Los Angeles, however, gaining entrée is next to impossible since most of the studios there are attached to major TV networks and movie sets.

Even if you're blessed with a good deal of willpower, security is tight, and only the right credentials or connections can get you inside.

As luck would have it, someone I knew was driving up to the studio gates where CBS programs were filmed and its local affiliate station's news broadcast was aired.

"Is that you?" she cried. "I can't believe it! How long has it been?"

Alma Pilar is a saucy, bouncy brunette who played a luckless role on *All My Children* and now portrayed a sexy, scheming femme fatale on *Falcon Crest*. We had met during my salad days in New York, when I interviewed her for *The Soap Box*. I was impressed by her grace, wit, and intelligence, as well as by her classy good looks. The daughter of a Mexican doctor and an American mother, she was bilingual and had received a law degree before beginning her acting career. We hit it off right away and stayed in touch for several years after I stopped working with the soaps. Still, we hadn't seen or spoken to each other in about five years.

"What in the world are you doing here, *sol de mi día?*" she asked, getting out of her red Mercedes convertible and leaning against its door. "Are you back in television again—writing or acting?"

No, I explained, I was here in Hollywood on other business. Could she help me get past the gatekeepers and into the newsroom?

"*Claro que sí,*" she replied, falling back into her car and answering me in Spanish. "*¡Vete conmigo!* I'll drop you off at the door."

Alma Pilar placed her moist palms on my cheeks and kissed me, continental style, on both sides of my face. Scribbling her phone number on a corner of the script she was carrying, she tore it off, tucking it gently into my hand and making me promise to call her before returning home.

* * *

The convention kept me busy the rest of the week, but, not having any plans for Friday evening, I called Alma on Thursday. We would be heading back east late on Saturday, I said. I'd love to see her, if she was available, the next night.

"Bruce, *mi amor,* you've got to come over. I'm having a party, and there are some people I think you'd like to meet," was her answer. "Should I send a car or do you have transportation?"

Thanking her for the invitation, I asked for directions.

The taxi wound its way up and around the steep Hollywood Hills until it came to a driveway aglow in soft outdoor lights. Alma Pilar's home was a Spanish style stucco fronted by the ubiquitous palm trees that seemed to grow everywhere.

Though the front door was ajar, I knocked several times. Nobody answered, so I let myself into the marble tiled entrance foyer.

Inside, I faced a large, step-down living room impeccably decorated with thick, cream colored carpet and fawn leather furniture. A huge canvas of Alma Pilar hung over a brick fireplace that spanned the entire length of one wall. Opposite the fireplace, sliding glass doors favored twinkling lights from the big city below. People spilled out of the room onto a deck that overlooked a pool and tennis court. A galaxy of famous faces beamed as I passed among the celebrities sitting, standing, speaking, smoking, eating, drinking, and dancing wherever I looked.

María Alica glided my way, her left arm comfortably girding the waist and her right hooking elbows with a handsome, sandy-haired, beachcomber-looking man I had seen many times on TV.

"Bruce, you made it," she effused. "I'm so glad you could come, *cariño.* Do you know TJ?"

"No," I said, extending my hand. "It's a pleasure to meet you. I've seen your work on television. Any plans for making a sequel?"

Releasing her hold on him, TJ took my hand between his. "The pleasure, my man, I hope will be entirely mine," he rasped hoarsely in a baritone that, along with the stubble lining his lips and unshaven chin, had become his trademark. "Let's get a drink. Had anything to eat yet?"

"I had dinner before coming here," I replied, "but a good, strong drink would be wonderful. Lead the way."

Transferring his grasp on Alma Pilar to me, TJ wrapped his arm across my shoulder and hugged tightly as we shuffled to the bar. "What'll it be, *hombre?* Name your medicine."

I asked him for a Bloody Mary, heavy on the Tabasco. The bartender handed the drink to TJ, who, in turn, held it out to me.

"*Salud,*" he toasted, his hazel eyes meeting mine. "You look like you need to loosen up a bit."

* * *

This was one sexy dude. Casually attired in a white muscle T-shirt and shorts that accentuated lean legs and flattered his well-defined biceps and triceps, TJ was about two inches shorter than me. His smooth skin with its light wisps of hair gracing strong arms had a bronzed hue that seemed ingrained, a natural tan quite different from the reddish-brown staining of many California sunbathers and their East Coast wannabes.

"Do I meet with your approval?" He winked, as I stopped myself from staring. He couldn't be coming on to me, I reasoned. It was common knowledge the man was an icon with a lady-killer reputation who had recently remarried his former wife.

"Where's your wife? Isn't she here?" I asked, regaining my composure.

"Nope, couldn't make it. Her loss, my gain," he murmured taking a throaty chug of his whiskey before changing the subject.

Over a series of drinks—I'd lost count of how many, but knew it was more than my limit—we spoke of mutual acquaintances, lamented the lack of privacy in the public eye, the snares of fame, and the snakes following fortune. Beginning to feel woozy from too much to drink, I steadied myself with one hand against the wall. TJ laughed and took the other.

"You need to lie down for a bit. Come on," he prompted, patting my fanny and escorting me toward the circuitous spiral staircase.

We climbed the steps slowly. At the top, TJ steered me into one of the guest bedrooms, where he took off my shoes and stretched me out on the bed. Through the haze of my stupor and darkened cast filtering the room, I could see heavy, Spanish-style furniture arranged in a masculine motif. It was a room made for men, a setting in which guys could be comfortable.

TJ sat down next to me on the edge of the bed and fished something out from his pants pocket. A match's momentary flicker and the sweet, pungent smell told me what it was. Placing the weed between his right thumb and pointer finger, he took a deep toke and offered it to me. I shook my head no.

"What's the matter, buddy?" he inquired, touching my face with his left hand. "Don't you get off by smoking . . . or does a different kind of joint turn you on?"

My eyes were closed, but I could hear his zipper being unfastened as TJ stood and shed his clothing. I had to look, even if my eyes still were swimming. The man was an Adonis, beautifully shaped and well endowed.

"You know, you're extremely sexy," he whispered, kissing the contours of my aroused body. "I'm going to take very, very good care of you and make you feel a whole lot better."

That he certainly did!

* * *

I no longer remember everything we did with each other or how long we were in bed together. Nor can I recall how I got back to my hotel from Alma Pilar's or whether I had even said goodbye to her. But I'll never forget my night with TJ and how much I reveled in his talented touch.

Flying back from Los Angeles to Washington's Dulles Airport the next afternoon, I couldn't shake the aftermath of that heady encounter. For the first time in my life, I had enjoyed being sexually active with another man—without feeling remorse or recrimination.

My life had taken me to a critical crossroad. The question now facing me was whether I would decide to make it a real turning point?

33

PHALLIC NARCISSISM

On my return from Los Angeles, I learned that Amanda had been caught shoplifting at Montgomery Wards, where she had taken Julianna to buy some school clothes. As was her way, the spoiled girl had made quite a scene, demanding Amanda to buy her this, that, and the other thing. Exasperated, Amanda stuck some merchandise in her pocketbook and was caught by security agents as she exited the store. She was escorted to the executive offices and interrogated by the head of security while they waited for the police to arrive.

I bailed her out and hired an attorney to plead her case. The lawyer advised us to get counseling; documenting the stress Amanda was under would bode well, he said, for convincing the judge to let her off with a slap on the wrist.

So, by hook and by crook, we were finally forced to discuss our problems with a trained therapist. Amanda spent several sessions alone with the counselor. Though divorced and remarried, he claimed to be a Christian. And Amanda seemed willing and ready to begin unburdening herself. After their third session, the psychologist asked me to join them. He was a nice enough guy, but I had to watch what I said. Any rehash of our problems told from my viewpoint resulted in Amanda's frigid silence inside the office and a nasty fight when we got outside.

Things got worse when I consulted the therapist without her. He agreed with many of the points I had made and implied that Amanda actually twisted some of his conclusions and recommendations. When confronted about these inconsistencies, she went off on a tirade. It just went to prove she was right: You couldn't even trust a Christian!

That concluded Amanda's sessions with the doctor. The time she'd spent with him may or may not have helped her to understand that marriage, especially a second one, had to involve compromise, but it did nothing to relieve my anguish. We had reached an impasse in our marriage, neither talking nor dealing with our problems.

And I still needed to come to grips with my personal dilemma.

My experience with TJ still fresh in mind, I kept thinking about him and how much I had enjoyed our erotic encounter. Not that Amanda and I were attempting many conjugal efforts anymore; she slept on her side of the bed and I slept on mine. The few times we tried, however, there wasn't any desire. The whole situation was futile, frustrating, and downright depressing.

I was in limbo, sitting on the fence, and desperately needed to make a decision. What should I do and whom could I turn to?

* * *

My only source of comfort (hah!) was the gym, where, three times a week, I exercised. Working out on the Nautilus circuit and lifting free weights produced a purgative effect as I battered my body and bent my besieged soul.

The health club was an oasis, a set of parentheses between blunders at the office and home. Some of the regulars I had befriended there referred to it as *Cheers,* a place where everyone knew your name . . . and your game.

SQUARE PEG IN A ROUND HOLE

How Ralph and I became friends, I can't remember. He certainly wasn't from my social set. A big, strapping guy who measured six-feet three inches and weighed more than 250 pounds, Ralph was the only person I've ever known to qualify as a Jewish-Italian. Like me, he grew up in New York. Before moving to Manassas, he had managed both a pizza parlor and a delicatessen. Now he worked as a construction superintendent. Ralph had been divorced several years and now had custody of his son, Marty, who was the same age as Jonah (they both were now nearly thirteen).

We would joke about stupid stuff that seemed appropriate at the time.

"If Jon Bon Jovi were here, I'd be the first in line to give him a blow job," Ralph once laughed, unaware, I had thought, of my sexual dichotomy. I later learned that he had participated in a *ménage à trois* with his best friend, a New York City policeman, and Ralph's wife. But I never asked him what role he played.

Sometimes the topics of our conversations were more serious.

Although I had hinted, off-handedly, about my marital problems, Ralph knew something was really wrong. After one of our workouts, we went for a beer and talked. Limiting our discussion to the conflicting interpretations Amanda and I had of a second marriage, Ralph asked me what she wanted.

"To be happy," I replied.

"And what do you want?"

"I want to be happy, too."

"So, what's the problem if you both want to be happy?"

"It's just that she expects me to be the source of her happiness," I said. "She believes it's my responsibility to keep her happy. *'Husbands, love your wives, just as Christ loved the church,'* she recites, meaning that I should sacrifice my happiness and put hers ahead of mine.

"The only trouble is that, to make Amanda happy, I end up unhappy," I said. "It's a paradox, and it just isn't working for either of us."

"Nobody can make another person happy," Ralph declared.

"If making her happy makes you that unhappy, then something's wrong. Are you supposed to be miserable for the rest of your life just so she's happy? Life's too short. Get a life, man."

So much for Ralph's advice. It didn't really help to resolve the circumstances, but he did make me feel a little bit better.

* * *

Suzanne was another special friend I made at the club.

Interestingly enough, I had first known her husband, Gary, since he worked out there, too, and we got to talking one day in the locker room.

Amanda and I met Gary and Suzanne at a gym-sponsored party. Two weeks later, Gary was gone, leaving Suzanne for another woman. I nursed her through the anger and grief, cheering as she grew stronger and more sure of herself. Sprite and agile, Suzanne taught elementary school and aerobics, and involved herself in various extracurricular activities: She attended seminars on positive thinking, and she belonged to the ski club and the local swing dance society. Through it all, she'd attracted a slew of admirers whose zany adventures one day would form the basis of a book we would write together.

Knowing how jealous Amanda could be, I hardly ever mentioned Suzanne or the friendship we'd developed. But that didn't stop me from talking about Amanda to my new female friend. Suzanne had little patience for my wife or her "unrealistic expectations." She commiserated with me and was the third person to suggest I make an appointment to see Connie Brown, a clinical social worker who had cornered the market on the club's shrink and counseling trade.

Consulting a woman about my masculine problems wasn't something I'd been willing to consider. Yet—especially after Amanda's tirade that, if I were a woman, I'd understand her position—I convinced myself that input on my marital difficulties from a qualified member of the opposite sex might be helpful.

SQUARE PEG IN A ROUND HOLE

* * *

A tall and striking blonde, Connie Brown was working on her third marriage. The failure of two previous marriages and the uncertainty of a third didn't inhibit her ability to zero in on some of my problems with Amanda as we dissected the marriage and its maelstrom of daily events.

"She's a whirlwind of chaos," Connie concluded following our first session, "while you crave calm waters and need a safe, sheltering harbor."

Right on, woman!

Connie certainly earned her fee during our second session together.

Why, I wanted to know, did I feel such a sense of trepidation every time I came home and inserted my key in the front door? Removing her spectacles, Connie peered at me and pronounced a verdict that would have done Freud proud.

"Could it be," she asked, preferring that I arrive at my own conclusions, "that there's something symbolic about it? Do you see any parallel between having sex with your wife and coming into the house through the front door?"

I left in a daze, realizing that Connie had hit upon a remarkable verity.

After six sessions—one attended by Amanda, who left in a huff when Connie asked her to explain something—we reached several conclusions, the most important being that I needed a break.

Whether or not the marriage would survive, I needed to be alone now. Advising that a separation would definitely be good for me, and maybe even for us, Connie ended our sessions. She hoped she had been helpful and encouraged me to make an appointment any time I ever wanted to talk.

"One last question before I leave," I asked, knowing that my 50 minutes were just about up. "Amanda resents that I have a new BMW while she drives an old Honda. Why is it so important for me to own a BMW?"

"Phallic narcissism," she smiled, opening the door for me to leave.

Laughing all the way out of her reception room and into the parking lot, I had difficulty inserting my key in the door lock.

Connie Brown drove the same car that I did!

* * *

My good mood didn't last very long. I was home in ten minutes and Amanda greeted me with sarcasm. "So what advice did the dragon at the gate give you this time? Was I dragged through the mud again, or did you to find something else worthwhile to discuss for seventy-five dollars?"

"Let's sit down and talk sensibly, without so much venom for a change," I said softly, determined to tell her I was going to move out for a while. I didn't know where I was going or when I'd be leaving, but it was obvious that nothing would improve by maintaining the status quo.

Attempting to inject some humor into a situation that wasn't at all funny, I took her hand as we sat down facing each other on separate couches in the living room. "You know," I began, "even our pets have problems surviving here."

I had always had pets and, until Amanda and her children moved in, I never had a dog that I couldn't train. When Amanda and I married, I wanted to get a Siberian husky. But she was unaccustomed to pets and begged me to get a "cute little puppy" so she could adapt.

"Please, honey," she begged during our second month of marriage, when life was still sweet and pleasant between us. "I've always wanted a shih tzu, but my mother never would let us bring a dog into her house. Let me get used to taking care of a small dog, a shih tzu, and then you can have a bigger one, if you want. The house is big enough for two, and the backyard's fenced in."

I gave in.

Training the dog occupying our premises was my responsibility. Her disposition was loving, but even without the children's constant yapping and pawing, her little constitution was quite fragile and "delicate." The tiny Shih-Tzu shit-zued all over the house!

Our second dog was a miniature collie, Amanda's next favorite breed. We followed ads in the newspaper until finding a five-month-old puppy that a breeder in Reston assured us was already trained. The dog threw up all over the back seat of my car as we headed home. Once there, she made a beeline for Amanda's closet. She extracted my wife's favorite red shoes and began chewing them, leaving tooth marks all over the heels. Amanda screamed at the dog, who jumped on our bed to urinate.

"Marking her territory," the experts called it, though the bed wasn't exactly her territory. From that moment on, the dog wouldn't eat anything but her own coat, nibbling away at her body.

"Bring her right back!" insisted the breeder, which we did, not a month after we got her.

The next specimen was a beautiful Siberian Husky I adopted from the pound. At ten months, Rocky had outgrown the apartment where his owners lived and made a habit of running away. After the third call from the animal shelter saying they had the dog, his owners told them to keep him. During his first month with us, Rocky was on his best behavior, and even Amanda fell in love with this handsome, noble gentleman. He romped in our backyard, sat on command, and slept on the floor at the foot of our bed.

Returning from work one evening, however, I found the house completely trashed. I screamed bloody murder at the dog, sticking his snout in the mess and yelling, "No! No!! No!!!"

The dog wouldn't take no for an answer. Day after day, we'd come home to find garbage strewn throughout the house, overturned objects, and broken bric-a-brac everywhere.

Amanda and I waited two months before we brought another dog into our home. This time we got a West Highland White, the same terrier breed

Barbara and I had successfully trained and coexisted with so peacefully. This time, there'd be no mistakes.

"Get a crate for housebreaking," suggested the pet-training books, explaining that dogs wouldn't defile their sleeping areas. We were to feed her small amounts of food every few hours and put her on paper, holding her there until she did her business.

Wouldn't you know it, Gretel was the one dog in a hundred that refused to be crate-trained! No matter how often she went when we put her on paper or placed her out back, she'd go again as soon as we returned her to the crate. She simply couldn't hold it in.

Gretel developed a fatal skin disease intrinsic to Westies. Much as we resented the extreme efforts we'd taken to train her, we really regretted following the veterinarian's advice and having her put to sleep.

She was the last dog to live under the same roof as Amanda and I.

34

LIFE'S A BITCH

"Are you calling me a bitch?" Amanda asked, quite annoyed with me. "You're not trying to compare me to a dog, I hope."

"Of course not. I'm just trying to sort things out, to find the right way to say what I have to, and help you to understand my feelings."

"You haven't slept with me since you came back from California. I think I've got a pretty good idea of how you feel . . . or how you don't now."

"No, you don't, Amanda," I stammered. "You really have no idea."

"Is there someone else? Are you involved with another woman? Is that what this is about? Or is there something else you haven't told me?"

"There's no other woman, I swear. It's me. The problem is with me."

"Then, what is it? Talk to me, Bruce. I think I have a right to know."

"Amanda, we're not happy. In case you haven't noticed, I've been going through a major depression. Yes, part of it is your fault, although much of it's mine. No, I'm not involved with anyone else. I'm not even certain I know what I want, anymore. But I have to find out."

"What's that supposed to mean? Tell me the truth, please. Have you been unfaithful? Did you sleep with another woman in California?"

"I didn't sleep with another woman . . ."

"So what's wrong? Why won't you make love with me?"

"Because I can't."

"Why can't you?"

"Because I think I may prefer being with a man."

The silence rebounded profoundly as Amanda tried to digest what I'd told her. "I don't believe you," she finally said. "It doesn't make sense. Not after all the times we've made love. You're making it up . . . it's your way of trying to get out of it. You're afraid to tell me our marriage is over. Isn't that it?"

"I'm sorry, Amanda, but it's true. I wasn't with another woman in California . . . I had sex with another man."

"You're sick," she shuddered. "If this is some kind of joke, I don't find it funny. I think you'd better let me alone now. I've got some thinking to do."

I slept in the guest bedroom that evening and left for my office early, before Amanda awoke. When I came home later in the afternoon, her bags were packed and set by the front door. "I'm going to visit my aunts in Boston for a few days," she stated mechanically. "The children will stay with John while I'm gone."

* * *

Amanda left for Boston on Thursday morning, and I decided to take advantage of the time alone. Friday evening, I got in my car and headed for Dupont Circle. There were plenty of opportunities in the area.

I parked somewhere on P Street and walked around for a while, peering into windows and trying not to stare at the men who strolled the streets, some hand-in-hand. Around eleven o'clock, I got up my nerve and ventured into Badlands. The place was dark and noisy, packed with pretty boys and brute butches on the make. I bought a Budweiser and sat at the bar, swiveling around on my stool to watch the cruising parade. Presently, someone shifted himself next to me and asked if he could buy me a drink. I checked him out, concluding he wasn't my type.

"No thanks," I said, holding up my full bottle and turning aside. He wouldn't leave. "Want to dance?" he continued. Shaking my head, I got up and moved away.

Now what? I checked out the back room where guys were watching videos and then went upstairs. A group of cross-dressers were shooting pool. At midnight, I made my way to a small anteroom behind the dance floor and sat in a corner, nursing my third beer.

From the corner of my vision, I noticed a sexy cowboy with a mustache whose eyes seemed to lock with mine every time I looked his way. He reminded me of Geraldo Rivera. After a while, he moseyed over and sat down beside me.

"Never liked playing cat-and-mouse games," he said. "My name is Stephen. And yours is?"

"Ummm . . . Bruce."

"Has anyone ever told you, Bruce, that you've got incredible eyes?"

Stephen and I measured each other against our own expectations. He was well built and rather good-looking, but it bothered me the way he lisped his words. It bothered him that I was married and out on the prowl.

The hour was late and he calculated, I guess, it was time to fish or cut bait. "Do you want to come over to my place?" he asked. "I live in Alexandria," less than 20 minutes away.

"Sure," I replied and followed him in my car.

Stephen was a hairdresser. His house was just around the corner from the successful shop he owned. He lit a fire in the hearth and handed me a beer as we sank onto the carpet and listened to Edith Piaf.

"My lover and I just split up after living together for four years," he told me. "You're the first guy I've been with and the only married man."

"My wife and I are about to be separated," I offered.

"Because of your sexual orientation?" he asked. "Does she know that you're gay?"

"I don't know if I am."

"Then what are you doing here?"

"Maybe I'm bisexual," I responded.

Stephen removed his hand from my pants leg and told me to call him after I'd made up my mind. "You can't have it both ways," he argued. "Neither can I."

Though disappointed that nothing more had come from that evening with Stephen, my decision to leave Amanda, to explore my options on the other side of the fence, had been reinforced.

* * *

Amanda returned from visiting her aunts after four days in Boston. She'd sorted things out and had made her decision. My wife wasn't ready to give up her meal ticket.

"This is totally new and unexpected," she informed me. "But you stood by me when I had that shoplifting trouble, and I'm willing to stay with you if you'll go to get help." She wanted me to seek counseling from Exodus International, an "ex-gay" ministry loosely affiliated with our church. I, however, wasn't ready to take such a step. Before exorcising any gay demons, I had to determine whether they were a curse or a blessing in disguise. And I couldn't do that until I knew for sure on which side of the sandwich my bread was buttered.

"I'm sorry, Amanda, but it just wouldn't work," I apologized. "I need the freedom to find out who I am, to figure out what I really want and need. It's impossible for me to do that while we're living together. I think a trial separation would be best for both of us."

Amanda pursed her lips and hardened her expression.

"So what do you propose? Where am I supposed to go? I can't move back in with my parents, and I don't have the money to go anywhere else—unless you're paying."

"You don't have to go anywhere," I said in a conciliatory tone. "The kids are in school here, and it wouldn't be fair to uproot them again. The problem is mine, so you can stay here. I'll move out."

"Where will you go?"

A good question, I thought. Renting an apartment was a waste of money. The cheapest place went for $700 a month and I'd be throwing it away. Neither did I want to rent a room, sharing space in a group home somewhere, since I needed my privacy. Besides, I had no idea how long it would take for me to reach my conclusions.

"I'm going to buy a condo," I told her matter-of-factly. "In the meantime, I'll sleep in the downstairs guest bedroom next to my study."

My grandmother had died recently and left me ten thousand dollars. I would use the money as a down payment on a place of my own. It would be an investment, I rationalized. Not only would there be tax advantages, I could sell or rent it when I determined what I wanted.

What was logical to me made no sense whatsoever to Amanda.

"I see," she answered. "Just like that you're going to buy a piece of property. It seems you've already made up your mind, Bruce. People who want to work on their marriage don't run out and buy a condominium. Whose name will it be in, yours or ours? How long do you plan to be there?"

"I'm not sure . . . maybe six months, perhaps longer."

"What am I supposed to do in the meantime? Just wait here until you decide if you want to stay married to me? And how am I going to afford living here alone with the children?"

"You'll manage," I said. "I'll continue making the mortgage payments. It'll be up to you to find a way to meet your other expenses. Maybe you can find a roommate."

"That's just great! Do you expect me to run an ad in the newspaper?"

"Why not? Lots of people do. In fact, I did, you know! I'll place the ad, screen the callers, and meet with them, if you want," I offered.

"No. I won't have a stranger living here with me and my children. Don't worry too much about us, faggot," she spat sarcastically. "I'm sure we'll find a way to manage without you."

* * *

Over the next few weeks, I scouted properties and found what I was looking for. "For sale by owner: Executive penthouse, two bedrooms, fireplace, washer & dryer, excellent condition."

The condominium belonged to two lesbians who had decided to go their separate ways after three years of living together. Their apartment had cathedral ceilings, skylights, a country kitchen, enclosed sunroom, and two bedrooms separated by the living room and a hallway that led to the bathroom. It had the same color carpet as my house and would make a perfect retreat for Jonah and a sanctuary for me.

I made them an offer. After some dickering, we agreed on a price and settled on a date six weeks away for closing. In the meantime, I bought the stuff that I would need—kitchen appliances, some wallpaper, linens and things. As each purchase was added to the guest bedroom where I was now sleeping, Amanda's mood turned from bad to worse. She refused to believe I actually was moving out.

Taking the guest bedroom set, family room furniture, dinette, my clothing, and recent purchases, I rented a U-Haul and enlisted the help of Ralph and several friends from the gym to help me move.

Not a week had passed after I moved out when I learned from a friend that Amanda met another man. I couldn't really blame her, nor was I in any position to point an accusatory finger. What was good for the goose was sauce for the gander.

In all honesty, I had mixed feelings about what was happening but knew in my heart that I'd made the right decision. Whatever else, Amanda's affair gave me license—and less guilt—to follow my own direction now.

35

Res Ipsa

Though I knew I was attracted to men, I couldn't get a grip on my peculiar sexual grid: Was I a conflicted heterosexual, a bisexual, or a gay guy who needed to be straight with himself and quit hiding and playing games in the closet?

Res ipsa: the matter speaks for itself, claim the wise doctors of jurisprudence. And, though not an attorney, I thought the Latin expression seemed to fit my dilemma, reflecting past and current choices, plus my new bearings.

Living on my own leveled the playing field and provided a proving ground. I now had the liberty—and opportunity—to satisfy my curiosity as well as to take appropriate action to liberate my libido.

36

BLIND DATES

How do you go about meeting compatible men with comparable orientations and interests if you're not into the bar scene, aren't yet ready for organized gay groups, and, after making eyes at strangers in subways, get off the train before it leaves the station?

The choices were limited and relatively cloistered, especially before graphic Internet Web sites and camcorders let it all hang out. "Hooking up" in chat rooms has become so easy now: simply point-and-click your way.

But I began by renting a post office box and then placing a blind ad in *The Washingtonian:* "BIWMM—Good-looking, sexy, seeks special buddy to explore mutual interests. Letter and recent photo appreciated."

My deliberate wording would let potential respondents know that I was married and, as yet, unwilling to go on the record as completely homosexual. Still uncertain about my sexual orientation, I believed I had more in common with married bisexuals than many gay blades.

Waiting for my announcement to be published, I answered a couple of ads appearing in the magazine's current issue. That's how I met Rod.

A month after I wrote him, he clipped his own ad and stapled it to my letter, which he returned with a photograph. "Sorry it's taken so long to get back to you," he'd hastily jotted in blue magic marker. "I've been out of town the last month and am only now getting around to catching up on my correspondence. If you're still interested in getting together, give me a call and leave a message on my voice mail."

According to the limited details he'd sketched, Rod was separated from his wife and two children, and he was two years younger than me. He said he was six-feet two inches tall and, if his formal picture wasn't too distorted or out of date, he'd be considered suitably attractive.

We played telephone tag several times before talking. Despite an amiable conversation, all he would tell me was that he'd returned to school after several years in a medical profession. Anything else would have to wait until we met in person. We set a date for 5:00 pm the following Friday, when we'd rendezvous in front of a bowling alley in Arlington.

Rod's picture was a good likeness. He had light brown hair and was obviously in good shape. Leaning against my car, I had no trouble spotting him heading in my direction as he walked across the parking lot.

We covered the basics in fewer than five minutes. Meeting me had heightened his interest in taking things further, he said. I, too, was willing to take the next step.

"Do you want to follow me back to my place?" I offered. "It's about a half hour's ride from here, more or less."

"You really must be new at this," Rod laughed. "You just don't meet a total stranger and immediately invite him to your home. What if I were a pervert, another Jeffrey Dahmer?" The gruesome serial murderer killed at least 17 men and boys between 1978 and 1991.

"Point well taken," I admitted. "So what do you suggest?"

Rod removed a day-timer with social calendar from his bowling bag. "How about getting together for dinner sometime next week? Thursday is good for me, if you don't have any plans."

"Thursday is all right by me, too. Someplace quiet? How about the Italian Inn on Route 50? It's midpoint between Washington and Manassas."

"Fine. I'll meet you there at six."

Before Thursday rolled around, however, I'd met someone else.

* * *

My ad in *The Washingtonian* had been published. In the first week alone, I received over a dozen replies. My heart beat wildly as I extracted the envelopes from my post office box and scurried to my car, clutching them like contraband.

Sitting in the parking lot, I ripped each one open and scanned the contents. Mail came from four married men, two Marines, a policeman and a number of gays, along with a damning warning from a vigilant Samaritan who said I was going to burn in hell for my sinful deeds. Why, I wondered, was he reading these classifieds?

Separating the envelopes between those that included photos and those that didn't, I placed a rubber band around them for more careful study later. One or two included fuzzy photocopies of pictures showing the sender's special assets in rather revealing positions. Over and over, I reread the letters. Each spoke of carnal desires and a need for gratification. Few indicated interest in developing a friendship; most wanted partners for an afternoon frolic. Only one message in the whole batch elicited my interest and prompted an instant follow-up.

Carefully clipped to the inside left corner of a note card written with precise, scrolling letters was a shirtless photo of a rugged individual signing himself Matt.

Matt described himself as an aging hippie, a Vietnam veteran who had once got it on with another solider when they were alone, stationed in a military bunker. He couldn't forget the experience and wanted to see, again, what it would be like to be with another man. The return address gave a post office box in Middleburg. Although he didn't live far from me, in Fairfax, he was spending a week doing a friend a favor—tending his farm in the horse country. If I was interested, I should call him before he left there on Sunday.

I did so immediately.

Admitting he'd had second thoughts after mailing the letter, Matt didn't seem too surprised to pick up the phone and hear me introduce myself. Like a hound after the fox, round and round we went during our thirty-minute conversation. Before being drafted for military service, he attended school in Boston and studied to be an architect. He never returned to college after the war and now did odd jobs here and there, waiting for that big break to make good on his fledgling artistic career.

In the meantime, Matt lived with his girlfriend of five years. Marion made the money as a successful systems analyst, working two weeks every month at her company's headquarters in Virginia and another two abroad at its London office. She was in London when we spoke and wouldn't be coming back for another week. "Could we, maybe, get together sometime before then?" Matt wanted to know.

Relying on my instincts, I disregarded Rod's dire warning and invited Matt over for dinner on Monday.

* * *

Dressed in blue jeans and a work shirt, he showed up five minutes early with a bottle of wine and bunch of roses from his garden. I took the flowers and told him to pour some wine while I fixed our dinner. Never adept at cooking, I thanked God for the local Giant grocery and the prepared foods available in its gourmet section. I nuked Chicken Cordon Bleu, baked potato skins with cheese, and heated up some asparagus. I'd also bought a loaf of fresh French bread and Napoleons for dessert.

"That was terrific," raved Matt, tilting his chair back. "Where did you learn to cook like that?"

"How about refilling our wineglasses and making yourself comfortable in the living room?" I asked, avoiding an answer. "Let me rinse off these dishes and put them in the dishwasher, then I'll join you."

Feet on the coffee table—he'd removed his sneakers—Matt was lounging on the couch, his left arm draped across its cushions. I sat down on the couch, but not next to him, and waited to see if he would make the first move. Unfortunately, he didn't.

We continued talking for about an hour, when Matt looked at his watch and said it was late . . . he'd best be going. I walked him to the door, thinking I'd missed my chance. He really was cute.

"Thanks for the evening," he said. "I had a good time."

"You're welcome, I'm sure. The feeling is mutual."

We stood there eyeing each other, before I got out my next two words. "Now what?"

Matt moved closer and kissed me on the mouth, his beard tickling my lips. He hugged me tightly, too.

"I wish you had come on stronger. I would have liked to see what could have happened," he ventured. "I guess we're going to have to get together again, if you want."

"I want! So, when?"

"Marion is coming home on Saturday. I have to pick her up at the airport. How does Friday sound to you? I'll bring over Chinese food."

"Looking forward to it," I said, squeezing his shoulder and shutting the door behind him. I heard him retreating down the stairwell, two steps at a time, the outside door creaking closed and then his motor rumbling.

Matt was gone before I realized I hadn't asked him for his number.

37

OSCILLATING CURRENTS

Dressed in a starched white shirt, tie, and double-breasted navy blue pinstripe suit, Rod was waiting for me when I arrived that Thursday at the restaurant. He had cornered a secluded booth on the far side of the room and took the liberty of ordering a carafe of red wine.

"You're right on time," he greeted me. "I admire that."

"How long have you been here?" I asked, now taking a closer second look. Rod was handsome, although I usually was drawn to darker features.

"I got here just about five minutes before you."

As we dawdled over dinner for the next two hours, I learned a little more about him and appreciated how much we had in common. Like me, Rod came from a Jewish background . . . I was from New York, he hailed from Chicago. He was a doctor of podiatry, but recently had sold his practice. Although separated, we both still were legally married.

Rod's wife and mine bore an uncanny resemblance—not only physically, but in their emotional composition. He had two young children; I had Jonah and two stepchildren courtesy of Amanda. Even our respective experiences with pets left a lot to be desired. While dogs had come and gone from my home, Rod was the one to leave because of the canine companions. His wife,

Wanda, bred Pekinese show dogs; seventeen of them now resided in their house.

Between feeding and breeding, bathing and brushing, the routine infringed on other aspects of Rod and Wanda's marriage.

"It's like an assembly line," Rod explained of the efforts involved in caring for them, "but I finally put my foot down when she asked me to masturbate them."

"What?" I choked, coughing on my wine.

Rod explained that, due to inbreeding and physical limitations, Pekinese evidently need some help in the mechanics of mating. He refused to participate in these machinations, so Wanda had turned to the "handyman," as Rod called him. Though the guy had been hired to repair the house, he now handled the dogs' daily needs, accompanying them with Wanda to the vet, groomer, and competitions. Spending so much time in their company, he later moved in.

Rod moved out and took an apartment in Georgetown. I suspected that money wasn't a problem, since he paid the high rent, as well as tuition at the law school he attended full-time. Rod had been with several men before me, he confessed, but wasn't willing or ready to commit to being AC or DC. In the meantime, he plugged his fan into oscillating currents. Yet he made an interesting comment that would haunt me as I wrestled with my own dilemma and course of action.

All things being equal, given the choice, he believed, most guys claiming to be bisexual would choose men over women.

Our dinner completed, Rod wanted to know if my invitation was still open. He was now ready to return to my place.

Watching him get out of his car when we parked in front of my condo told me a lot about Rod's personality. He carefully removed clothes covered in a garment bag hanging on a hook in the back seat, then opened the trunk and took out a traveling cosmetics case. In it, I later learned, were a comb and hairbrush, toothpaste and toothbrush, dental floss, mouthwash, a razor and shaving cream, shoe stretchers, rubber bands, condoms, and two bottles of cologne. Rod must have been a Boy Scout; he sure came prepared.

Upstairs, I directed him to put toiletries in the bathroom and hang his clothes in my bedroom closet. Rod methodically removed his suit jacket, tie, and pants, hanging them on their own padded hanger. He unbuttoned his shirt and neatly folded it, undoing the creases before laying it on my dresser. Off came his socks, cotton briefs, and undershirt, which were tucked into a plastic bag for laundering. Inserting stretchers in polished shoes, he then settled down and we got into bed.

That was the first time I'd spent a night with another man, awakening the next morning to find him there in my bed. Rod showered while I put up some coffee. Then I stumbled into the bathroom, while he slipped out for a few minutes to buy bagels and cream cheese from the corner convenience store. Having breakfast together was a pleasant experience.

Saying he'd call me over the weekend, Rod left for home and I went off to my office. He was a neat guy, I had to give him that, but there weren't any fireworks between us. Comparing my feelings about Rod and Matt, I knew I had more in common with one but a greater intensity for the other.

* * *

Matt arrived early with two bags of Chinese food in hand.

"This will keep. They said we can reheat it," he grinned as he dropped the bags on my kitchen table. "Why don't we have dessert first and then eat our entree?"

The man was truly insatiable. Unlike Rod and his meticulousness, Matt kicked off his sneakers, casually pulled off his polo shirt and dropped his pants, letting them fall haphazardly to the floor. He stretched out on the bed, arms tossed and tangled at right angles covering the pillows.

With his bristly beard, warm and furry belly, his doleful brown eyes and mop of unruly hair, Matt was truly adorable and reminded me of a big, shaggy mutt.

We finally got around to eating our dinner at eleven o'clock.

"It's been fun, but I have to get back home in case Marion calls from London," he said, getting up from the table and ambling to the door. "I'm not into one-night stands, so I hope we can schedule a repeat performance."

"When did you have in mind?"

"Marion is going to Philadelphia for the day a week from tomorrow. How about if I come over next Saturday afternoon?"

"What time?"

"About two?"

"That'll work. But before leaving, would you mind giving me your number?"

Shifting his eyes to avoid a direct answer, he fumbled, "I'd rather not, if you don't mind. It's kind of complicated with Marion."

"Matt, I'm not planning to call you just to chit-chat. What if something comes up, and we need to change our plans?"

"It won't," he insisted.

But it did.

* * *

Just after noon on Saturday came a hesitant knock of knuckles rapping on my door. Expecting to see Matt earlier than expected, I opened it without asking who was there. I was flabbergasted to find Craig McAllister standing in my doorway.

"What're you doing here, Craig?" I asked. "How did you know where I live?"

Smiling with those gorgeous dimples, square jaw, and cleft chin, he replied, "I stopped by your house and your wife told me. She said you were separated."

"Yes, we are. How is it that you seem to turn up, unexpected, whenever I'm in the midst of marital turmoil? It's been two years since you disappeared on me and I haven't heard a word."

"Mental telepathy?" he grinned, turning on the charm.

Those two years had been good to my former student. Though still somewhat flippant, he had matured from a cocky schoolboy into a model man exuding sex appeal that would make even *GQ* and *International Male* editors drool.

"What do you want and why are you here?"

"Can I come in?"

Leading him to the living room, he made himself comfortable on the couch. He took out a cigarette and asked, "Mind if I smoke? Do you have a match?"

I flicked my bic and told him to get on with it.

"Look, I'm really sorry about what happened. I just wasn't ready to deal with it then. The whole thing took me by surprise and I didn't know how to handle it. I guess I just got scared."

"So you disappeared? Come on, Craig, don't give me that bullshit. It takes two to tango, and you knew what you wanted then, as you do now. So, tell me, to what do I owe this dubious honor?"

"I'd like to do it again."

"Do *what* again?"

"Who's giving whom the bullshit, now?"

"And what makes you think I'm interested in that anymore?"

"Are you?"

"I might be, but I don't think with you."

"Why not?"

"Because you're a prick, and a thoughtless one at that."

"Won't you give me another chance? I've been thinking about you and that one night, and it always turns me on."

"Then go home and beat off."

He waited another minute before touching my arm. I melted and knew he'd have his way.

"Let's go into the bedroom," I motioned.

Turning away from me and toward the shaded window, he stripped off his clothes and got into my bed, where he retreated under the covers. I pulled off the comforter and had a good look; he was magnificent, and, you guessed it, I lost all self-control. But just as I began to unbuckle my belt and take off my shirt, someone began banging loudly on the front door.

"Who's that?" Craig gasped, bolting from the bed.

"I haven't a clue. Just be quiet and get back into bed. Whoever it is will think nobody's here and go away."

But the beating didn't stop. "Shit," I realized, "it's Matt."

"I've got to get out of here," groaned Craig, as he gathered his clothes and threw them back on. "What are you going to say? How are you going explain me being here like this?"

"Take it easy, Craig. It's not the problem you think it is."

"I don't want anyone to know about this. Please, promise me you won't say anything."

"Okay, don't worry," I assured him, straightening my clothes and combing my hair. "Go outside and wait on the balcony."

I then opened the door to Matt's hulking stance.

"What took you so long, man? Where've you been? I've been huffing and puffing and getting ready to blow the door down," he greeted me, walking in.

"We've been in the Florida room. I didn't hear you."

"Who's we?"

"One of my former students is here. He wanted my advice on reworking his résumé," I answered. "Come out and meet him."

Nervously, Craig stood up and shook Matt's hand. "Nice meeting you," he mouthed. Turning to me, he said, "Thanks for your help. I have to get going."

Leaving Matt on the sun porch, I walked Craig to the door.

"Sorry about the way things turned out, or didn't. Another time?"

"Yeah, sure, maybe. Who's he?"

"Matt's a friend from the health club. He's looking for a new job and needed some help putting his résumé together."

The little lie worked both ways.

"Great looking guy," Matt acknowledged when I returned. "Are you sure all you were helping him with was his résumé?" I laughed at the irony.

Matt didn't know about Rod and vice versa.

While neither, I presumed, suspected the other's presence, I continued seeing Matt and Rod for about six months, juggling my date-book to accommodate both. Rod and I had developed a special friendship, based on all we had in common. My relationship with Matt was purely physical.

Over the course of time, my involvement with Matt began to fade. He wasn't available when I was, and I resented his relationship with Marion. It wasn't that I was jealous—I still needed my freedom and wasn't ready to make a commitment—but it really annoyed me that he didn't trust me enough to divulge his address or phone number. Whatever was between us revolved around his convenience, and I was beginning to feel used. Matt announced he was going to Vermont for a few weeks to help two of his brothers with work on the family home. I never knew when or if he returned; I just didn't hear from him again.

My relationship with Rod was starting to ebb, too.

38

MÉNAGE À TROIS

One Saturday morning after Rod had spent the night, Barbara stopped by to drop off Jonah for my weekend with him. She brought along her friend Faith to keep her company.

Faith was tall and slim with long, blonde hair. From what Barbara said, many men found her attractive. Although she didn't appeal to me, apparently she did to Rod. I did the honors, introducing everyone around. Rod asked me what I knew about Faith after she and Barbara left.

Thus began a new chapter in my own, personal soap opera.

It started when Barbara and I arranged a double date one weekend. My ex-wife and I were on much better terms now that time had passed since our divorce and I'd separated from Amanda. Apart from her eating habits, we felt quite comfortable with each other. The four of us met for drinks at Rod's Georgetown apartment, then went out to eat . . . Barbara still sticking to salad. After catching a movie at an in-town cinema, we returned to Rod's and said our good-byes. Except for Faith.

"I really like her," Rod told me the next day, recounting what had happened. "She's a lot of fun, and I needed to know I can still perform with women in bed."

"Can you?"

"I was nervous and had some difficulty, but Faith was understanding—she attributed any problems to my divorce—and very patient with me. She obviously has experience and knew what she was doing."

"Are you going to see her again?"

"I'm not sure yet, but we discussed going to the beach one weekend. Her folks have a place in Ocean City."

From then on, I shared Rod's time with Faith instead of splitting mine between him and Matt. Turnabout being fair play, our roles were now reversed. He swapped partners and stole time together with me. The plot was thickening.

On Memorial Day weekend, Faith invited me to join Rod and her two children at her family's Ocean City beach house. Barbara, of course, was coming, as was Jonah. Her brother would be joining us there, too. Eight people in all would be stuffed into a one-bedroom bungalow three blocks from the water.

To say that the weekend was interesting would be to do it a grave disservice. One incident, in particular, stands out: Rod's sister also was spending the holiday weekend in Ocean City . . . not with us, but at a nearby hotel. She stopped by to say hello and meet us. Rod handled the who's whose. Her head seemed to spin, trying to keep the relationships straight.

"It's more convoluted than *Dynasty* or *Dallas,*" she said.

"Lady, if you only knew," I thought, as Rod caught my eye.

* * *

Barbara hoped the weekend vacation might add a bit of salve to our mortally wounded marriage. Lately believing in the importance of sticking together, no matter what the problems, she now regretted not working harder to salvage our connection. Although part of me still loved and cared about her, there were too many problems separating us to heal the strained schism.

"Why can't we even try?" she asked.

"Because we've gone our separate ways, changed, and become very different people now," I said.

Her eating habits gnawed at me. Though she weighed a mere 87 pounds now—dropping from juniors and petites to children's-size clothing—Barbara refused to eat anything but bird seed and rabbit food.

"Barbara, I just can't deal with the whole eating issue anymore."

"Why is that so important?" she asked. "Why must it matter so much to you?"

"When I care for someone, Barbara, I feel responsible—especially if I'm married to her. How can I be responsible for you if you won't take care of your own health? That's the first reason. Another is that eating is very important to me. I enjoy the social setting of going out for dinner. And I refuse to only eat in restaurants that specialize in salad bars."

At least, that part was true. But there was the other matter, too.

My life was complicated enough at the moment, trying to find its compass direction. I wasn't about to jump out of a scalding frying pan to blister myself in another fiery pot. I'd just freed myself from my second wife and wasn't interested in a replacement. Especially not the original model.

Nonetheless, I still did go out with a couple of women. I needed reassurance they found me attractive and wanted to determine whether I could still satisfy them (and me!) sexually.

They did; but I couldn't.

39

FRIENDS AND LOVERS

Jennifer was a beautiful blonde enrolled in both of the college courses I was teaching. Though she'd smiled at me throughout my lectures, nothing more happened until the end of the year, when she turned in her final exam. On top of her paper, she'd written, "Can you meet me outside?" Closing the door between the classroom and us, I asked what she wanted. She handed me a note in a scented pink envelope, imploring me not to read it until later, after leaving the campus.

"Now that I'm graduating and no longer your student, I'd like to invite you out to my place for dinner," she wrote.

I was floored but quite flattered.

Jennifer lived in a converted carriage house on a country estate about a 30-minute ride from my condo in Manassas. She was only 22, but I was impressed with her maturity and sophistication.

"What famous people would you most like to meet?" I baited her.

"Woody Allen, Mahatma Gandhi, and probably, Bob Dylan."

Even if she rattled those names off just to impress me, the girl was surely smart and had her act together. We enjoyed a leisurely dinner and returned to her place in the country where she excused herself to slip into something more comfortable.

We nestled together on the couch when she returned, kissing and petting until she wanted more. Not knowing whether I could deliver the goods, I made an excuse and sped back to Manassas. Before leaving, however, I asked her out again. It was dangerous, but I reciprocated and invited her to my place.

"Am I invited to stay over the night?" Jennifer asked that evening, after we had returned from dinner and a movie. Anxious to see if I still had what it took, I handed her a long T-shirt to sleep in and then deftly slipped it off.

Any other man would itch to devour her, but I could do no more than scratch the surface. Arduously, I stroked her luscious body, making her writhe as I tentatively touched its erogenous zones.

Jennifer probably thought the problem was a fear of getting involved.

"I have been very pensive about the situation and feelings resulting from our time together," she wrote in a letter mailed to me two days later. "I, too, am scared and confused about where this relationship will (or won't) go and where it should be headed.

"The purpose of this note," she concluded, "is to tell you that your fears and concerns are mutually felt. I am scared, excited, confused, and desirous. Let's try to take this one day at a time; no expectations, fears or attachments. We can have some fun, enjoy each other, and let whatever happen happen."

What happened was that I nipped any buds before they could blossom.

Apologizing for letting things get out of hand, I confessed to not being in a position to accept the generous terms of her offer. I wouldn't be able to live with myself by taking advantage. As impressed as I was with her maturity and finesse, the 20-year age difference between us was more than I, in good conscience, could handle. She was fabulous, beautiful, sensitive, and smart—with healthy desires normal for her age—and she unquestionably deserved more than I was able to give. Certain she would meet a man more worthy, I thanked her for caring and wished her well.

* * *

SQUARE PEG IN A ROUND HOLE

My other date was different, although its conclusion was the same.

"There's someone I want you to meet," prodded Suzanne, my friend from the health club. "She's your type: dark, very pretty, creative, and sharp as a tack. She's got a successful career, and I think the two of you will hit it off."

"How old is she?" I asked, reminding Suzanne of my latest fiasco but making no mention of my lack of desire to be fixed up with women.

"Your age, maybe a year or so younger."

"What does she do?"

"She's vice-president of an advertising agency in Bethesda."

"And why do you think she's interested in meeting me?"

"Sometimes you're really dense. You're handsome and smart, with a great personality. What woman wouldn't be interested? She asked me if I knew any eligible men. It took me two seconds to come up with you."

"You're sure she's not a dog?"

"Would I do that to you, Bruce? I know you're hung up on looks. Believe me, she's stunning."

"All right. Give me her number. I'll call and we'll see what happens."

Sheila and I hit it off on the phone and made plans to meet soon for dinner. Stunning she wasn't. Reasonably attractive, perhaps, and definitely worth a second glance. The way she sized me up across the restaurant table made me uncomfortable, and our conversation was stilted, at best.

Recapping the evening's events with Suzanne, I learned about the real reason for my discomfort the next day.

"What did you think of her? Did you have a good time? Was I right about Sheila being your type? Tell me what happened, I want to know everything!" she gushed over the phone the next morning, all in one breath.

"Not so fast, Suzanne. Have a heart," I begged. "It's still early, and I haven't yet had my morning coffee. First tell me what she told you. Then I'll give you a full report from my side of the story."

"I haven't heard anything from her yet. Sheila sleeps till noon on the days she's not working."

"So call me back after you two talk."

Several hours later, Suzanne called me again. This time, however, she wasn't so quick on the draw or eager to talk.

"What's wrong?" I inquired. "Bad news from Sheila?"

"No, not exactly . . . she said she had a nice time. But . . ."

"But what?"

"Sheila said there just wasn't any chemistry."

"She's right."

"She said something else, too, but it's really none of my business."

"Spit it out, Suzanne."

"Are you sure you want to hear this?"

"I wouldn't ask you to tell me if I weren't interested."

"Sheila thinks you're gay."

Not knowing how to respond to that, I waited for her to continue.

"Are you? Are you gay?"

"Does that matter to you, Suzanne?"

"Not to me. You know that I love you, no matter what."

"And if I am?"

"That's your business. Whatever turns you on and makes you happy is fine by me. I just don't want to put my friends in an awkward position by trying to play matchmaker for them if there's no point or way it can work."

"Understood," I replied. "So, then, this will be the last time you try to fix me up?"

40

LOST AND FOUND

That Suzanne's friend thought I came across as gay was a real revelation. How many other people, I wondered, were under the same impression? Not that it mattered anymore.

My forays with women and men had been equally frustrating.

I couldn't get it up for the former and, more often than not, couldn't commit to the latter . . . even though there was only Rod now.

And our relationship, what was left of it, didn't last much longer.

On Yom Kippur, the holy day of atonement when Jewish people beg God's forgiveness for their sins and another year with their names written in the Book of Life, Rod was expecting me over to spend the night. He would first be attending services with his family, but he had given me the keys to his condo. I was to let myself in, get comfortable, and wait for him.

Though no longer religious in the Jewish sense, my conscience bothered me and I was beset by guilt. I hadn't yet grappled with the matter of Christianity and homosexuality, or reached any conclusions as to what Scripture actually said about the issue. Were they mutually exclusive?

I took Rod's keys and put them in an envelope, along with a note of apology. "I'm sorry, but I can't be with you anymore," I wrote. "In the spirit of this holy day, please forgive me."

BRUCE H. JOFFE

Rod was pissed. He couldn't understand my change of heart or spiritual conflicts and was upset that I'd entrusted his keys to the U.S. Postal Service. What if they got lost?

The keys found their way. Now I needed to find mine.

41

ANOTHER MILESTONE

It was time to seek professional advice and try counseling again. But not with Connie Brown. My confessions couldn't be to a woman. I needed to speak to someone with the same biological equipment who could relate to my concerns.

Turning to the telephone book, I scanned the "Psychologists" listings, looking for men whose practice specialized in sexual dysfunctions.

The three psychologists I consulted—let's call them Larry, Curly, and Moe—held various outlooks and different therapeutic approaches.

- Dr. Larry was an elderly gentleman who talked more than he listened and loaded his monologue with jargon and psychobabble. His analysis prescribed intensive therapy thrice weekly to determine the roots of my problem. It absolutely, positively, could be traced back to my childhood.
- A Jewish man about my age from New York City with medical credentials, Dr. Curly preferred to dispense drugs for depression, along with bombastic bromides of advice. "To thine own self be true," he pontificated.
- Dr. Moe's perspective followed a more remote route. Dreams and fantasies, he believed, held the key to our health and well-being.

"Whom do you fantasize about," he asked me, "men or women?" By aligning—melding—extrinsic circumstances with our intrinsic passions, maintained Moe, conflicts were mitigated, confusion relieved, and reality was ultimately achieved.

I thanked each well-meaning adviser with a handshake and my check. But the real check on reality was being cashed by my own transactions, as I considered the few nuggets of wisdom I had mined from their sessions. "Whom did I fantasize about?" I already knew the answer to that question. It all now came down to doing what Dr. Curly had prescribed: "To thine own self be true."

It didn't take long to reach a conclusion and make my decision. While not yet ready to come out of the closet and march in Pride parades, I knew I was attracted to men more than women. That step in my journey to self-awareness realized, it was time to undertake a number of changes.

The first thing I did was to contact Amanda. I wanted a divorce, and we had to reach a settlement. Following a year's separation without cohabitation, it should be relatively quick and easy to arrange.

Silly me . . . nothing ever is that simple.

42

WAYFARER

Yep. Hell hath no fury like a woman scorned. Before losing her meal ticket, Amanda determined to keep our marriage alive with final, desperate measures.

Wearing nothing under her long, leather jacket, she showed up unannounced at my condo literally dressed to kill. A black widow spider to the fly? When that didn't work, she made an appointment to have her hair cut by Stephen, whom I'd been with only once and hadn't seen in many months. I have no idea how she found out about him, but assuming he was her rival, she wanted to assess the competition. She told him that I was married and that he couldn't have me because I belonged to her.

Poor Stephen. He probably didn't even remember me, but had to contend with a bat out of hell.

Next, she made phone calls and more personal visits.

She told her parents about my problem, which now had become hers. Amanda contacted my friends, namely Tom and Rosie Greene. She got in touch with my first wife to find out if she was aware of my deviant behavior.

Barbara refused to believe her.

Amanda made an appointment to meet with Andrew, the priest who had married us. He called me the next morning to ask if we could have lunch.

"Bruce, there's one important difference between your two weddings," was Andrew's position about the sanctity of marriage. "You weren't a Christian when you wed Barbara, but you were with Amanda. Jesus, himself, was there as a witness to your vows."

To appease Andrew—not Amanda—I agreed to one last stab at marriage counseling, at the offices of a respected Christian clinic. After ten sessions, they concluded we were incompatible and agreed about the logic of ending our marriage.

"How can you call yourselves Christians and yet approve of divorce?" Amanda challenged them. "Doesn't the Bible say God hates divorce: 'What God hath joined together, let no man put asunder?' Didn't Jesus morally condemn it as wrong? Divorce is a sin, and I can't believe I'm sitting here and listening to you condone it."

"Divorce isn't acceptable under most ordinary circumstances," they answered her. "Marriage was blessed by God because it can reflect the relationship between Christ and the church. But, sometimes, we take the wrong partner or marry for the wrong reasons. God wants what's best for us. In some cases, that means we're better off apart."

My spirit lifted, I took their words as gospel and took steps to finalize our separation. I filed divorce papers, listed the condo for rent or sale, and informed Amanda that I was moving back into my house.

* * *

In the five years I'd owned my home in Manassas, Barbara and I moved in . . . she moved out . . . and roommates moved in and out. When we reconciled, my tenants switched residences with Barbara; they moved into her place and she returned to mine. After ten months of the reconciliation not working, Barbara moved out again and another set of roommates joined me. A short time later, Amanda and I married. Once again my roommates moved out, to make way for my new wife and her children. Following four years of marriage, I had left, leaving Amanda and her children there. Now I was returning to evict them.

But I soon learned you never can really go back.

It didn't take me long to feel like I was living on *Knot's Landing*—all eight neighbors on the cul-de-sac knew my business; my comings and goings, guests, and companions. Another place, I hoped, would help me make a fresh start.

I sold the split-level and bought a new townhouse nearby. Eagerly, I anticipated putting my house in order and beginning a new life.

Two roads diverged in a wood, and I—I took the one less traveled by, and that has made all the difference, wrote Robert Frost. The words of his verse finally had hit home.

Forty years it had taken me to reach this diverging fork in my road. I wasn't going to waste any more time as a wayfarer aimlessly wandering this way and that.

43

CRUISING CONNECTIONS

Fairy tales can come true.

Through the portal into enchanted lands I hopped, peering at queer images projected by the carnival's looking glass. Along the way, I met white rabbits, mad hatters and march hares, queens of hearts, Cheshire cats, and white knights in drag.

Scheduling dinners and making appointments to meet men for drinks on week-nights, I juggled multiple meetings on weekend afternoons and evenings. Determined to make up for lost time, I dated with a vengeance.

Where did I find them? This was before AOL, gay.com, and M4M chat rooms, where immediate hook-ups can be negotiated after a few first "Sups?" "Stats?" "Intos?" and pics are exchanged.

Back then, I cruised the clubs, made telephone contact through the interactive connections I had discovered in the *Washington Blade* and *City Paper,* and responded to new ISO ads in *The Washingtonian.* I met a man on the street once, and found myself following cars with rainbow stickers.

I toyed with the club barflies, as we checked out the merchandise and scouted potential partners. Some still stand out, and I can remember their names; others I no longer choose to recall. It doesn't take long to learn you're better off forgetting about some of the scum that's hanging around out there.

* * *

Wayne, a gynecologist, lived in a large Gaithersburg townhouse decorated by his mother. His amber eyes glinted as he confessed more interest in the husbands who brought their wives into his examining room than any expectant women. Handing me his number, Wayne invited me to stop over. But he was too caught up in waiting for his dachshund to whelp, so it would have to be postponed a week or two.

Sorry, Charlie, I wasn't into waiting.

Then there was Carl, a short butch guy with a big, hairy chest. Shirt unbuttoned down to his navel, Carl strutted his stuff and swaggered right over in a dimly lit bar. I let him grab; he let me touch. Amazingly, Carl lived only a mile from me in Manassas. Making me promise to call him so we could get together, he jotted his number on a matchbook cover and stuck it into my pocket. He had come in a friend's car that night, and I offered him a ride home. But before I pulled out of the parking lot, he'd already split. Figure it out, if you can.

The list went on . . .

The Baltimore condominium maintenance man—suave and sophisticated—who appeared to be ten years my senior rather than five years my junior. The opera singer who looked like Pavarotti; he lived in a charming Georgetown duplex and prepared me a gourmet dinner. The apartment manager I met for drinks and then went back to his place for more. But when he got me into the bedroom, I just couldn't go through with it. Making excuses about this being my first time, I zipped myself up and left in a hurry. The University of Virginia senior so big, black, and smooth. He followed me home, where we sat talking in the living room until he wanted to go upstairs and take a bedroom tour. I wasn't really into it, so I showed him the front door.

* * *

More intriguing than these entanglements were the curious people I came to know through their canned introductions courtesy of the *Blade* and *City Paper*.

Here's how it works:

First, you write an ad, which—if you get it in by Monday—appears under the "Men Seeking Men" subheading in the next edition on Friday. At five dollars for up to 100 words, it's a bargain . . . but the deal gets even better.

You're assigned a voice mailbox number and told to record a two-minute greeting, telling more about yourself and the kind of person you're seeking. That part's free. Readers interested in responding to your ad call a 900 number and pay 99¢ a minute for the privilege of getting into your box. If they like the sound of your voice or the tone of your spiel, they'll leave a message. Retrieving any messages left for you is done by dialing a toll-free number and entering your own secret password.

Heart racing and adrenaline rushing, you hold your breath and wait for the mechanical recording: "There are *no* messages in your mailbox at this time" or "You have *X number* of new messages in your mailbox now."

Pen and paper in hand, you play back the messages, noting caller comments and scribbling down their words. They leave their telephone numbers, and it's your turn to call back any who seem promising.

Then the interview process begins. Depending on what you're looking for and want to know—who they look like, what they enjoy, when they're available, where they work, why they responded to your particular ad—you ask dumb questions like, "Which celebrity do people say you remind them of most?"

If both of you are interested in meeting, you set a time and a place to get together. That's when the real game of truth or consequences begins. One man's throwaway is another man's treasure; I suppose that's why so few people are honest about their looks.

One lesson I learned is that guys who say they're "very good-looking" usually are somewhat; those advertising themselves as "good-looking" without any superlatives attached more often are average. And anyone who describes himself as "attractive" probably isn't at all! More than one man I met through my paper capers fell into this last category.

Andy worked for the National Trust for Historic Preservation and promoted himself as attractive. When I pulled up to get him—we'd agreed to go to a movie—I found a guy with long, greasy, blond hair (what was left of it) tied in a ponytail, bad skin, and tattered jeans. I excused myself to go to the rest room and ducked out of the theater.

All things considered, however, this way of meeting men with similar interests, for me, at least, was better than the bar scene and certainly an improvement over most blind dates. Over the course of six months, it gave me the opportunity to associate with more than a dozen guys.

* * *

Bachelor number one was Eric Ramrod. How's that for a name! He compared himself to Kevin Costner, only better looking, and I was pleasantly surprised to find out his hype wasn't exaggerated. Meeting for lunch at the Key Bridge Marriott, each was impressed with the other's packaging. Eric came to dinner two days later—and then came again in my bedroom after eating.

Kevin was one of the sexiest men I'd ever seen. Affluent—he lived off his investments and drove a white Cadillac coupe—and gorgeous, he was a dead ringer for Pierce Brosnan, except somewhat scruffier. He announced he wasn't interested in a relationship; what he wanted was to fill his directory with numbers he could call when *he* was in the mood. Much as I would have liked to get to know him more intimately, we cut short our dinner and I showed him the way out. I refused to be just another number in anyone's little black book.

Michael also was a one-nighter. At first, I didn't return the message he left in my mailbox because he sounded a little too girlish. Lacking anything better to do one evening, however, I did end up calling. After all, he described himself as masculine and very handsome. As it turned out, voices can be deceiving. Michael was extremely good-looking and impressively built. It would have been my pleasure to see him again. Trouble was, he had just broken up with a lover of several years. Before trashing the relationship, however, he wanted to give it one more shot. I guess they worked things out, because he never called me back.

I don't mean to come across sounding so snippy. It's not that I'm under any superiority complex; I'm just persnickety and do set certain standards. Wasn't it Olympia Dukakis's character in *Steel Magnolias* who keenly observed, "The only thing that separates us from animals is our ability to accessorize"?

Mark was a nice little accessory. Short—five feet, six—with a head full of dark, curly ringlets, he was an endocrinologist who headed a Johns Hopkins research team studying the role of vitamins in disease prevention. Along the way, he'd learned a good deal about AIDS. Among homosexual men, he said, the primary cause of the virus—accounting for more than 98% of all cases—is unprotected anal sex. That wasn't something I was into, so I felt a little better about what I *was* doing.

Like many men looking for a little side action through these phone ads, Mark was married and maintained a private telephone number for his personal purposes. He claimed wifey knew about his dalliances and diversions but, for whatever reasons, she was willing to overlook them. I still find that hard to believe. Miriam was an orthodox Jew who insisted her family observe the Sabbath each Friday evening. Oh, that's right—Mark and Miriam had three children. We got together maybe two or three more times before I told him I was uncomfortable in the role of the "other person" involved in an adulterous affair.

You lose some, you win some; yeah, that's the way it goes. It was only a matter of days until I met someone else.

44

Limericks

A few minutes early for a downtown business meeting at Fifteenth Street and Eye ("I" to all but the locals), I sat on a park bench sipping some coffee when along came a spider who sat down beside me and gave me the eye.

"Nice threads," he commended of my Brooks Brothers suit and tie.

"Thanks. Glad you like them," I replied, taking in this total stranger. With light brown hair falling over his forehead and those cornflower eyes, he could have been the all-American boy next door. Only he wasn't.

"I'm Scott," he added, holding out his hand.

"Bruce," I supplied.

"Nice to meet you, Bruce. Do you come here often?"

"Not really. I have an appointment with one of my clients, but I'm a little early so I decided to kill some time."

"What do you do?" he inquired.

"Public relations. And you?"

"I'm working for a temporary service but interviewing for a job."

That explained why Scott Kramer seemed so impeccably groomed. Wearing a double-breasted blazer over a vest and white shirt, his Windsor-knotted tie was a subtle color that matched muted socks in shoes shined to a fine gloss. He was handsome, so I gave him my business card with phone and fax numbers before leaving for my meeting.

The next morning, our receptionist handed me this faxed message:

> *There once was a guy named Bruce/Who sometimes would act like a goose/But then he'd give you a hug/while down on the rug/and you couldn't make him mad!*

I fired off my own ditty to the fax number listed on the cover sheet:

> *Along came a man named Scott/who said, "I'll give this my best shot"/Alas, he was missing/those things that need kissing/but boy was he hot!*

Scott was ten years younger than I, but said he liked "older" men. He shared a floor in a Dupont Circle row house with several friends, which reduced his rent while job-hunting. He had managed an air courier company until he was let go when the firm was acquired by a larger competitor. Still seeing myself as lifeguard and caretaker, I helped him revise his résumé and delighted in the limericks we transmitted to each other daily.

Scott: *There once was a guy I call Pop/who said he was tough as a cop/He'd take out his "gun"/we'd have some fun/and then out of his place I would hop!*

Me: *Attempting to help Mr. Kramer/we professionally prepared this here paper/It's transmitted by fax/so he can relax/and get on with his career caper.*

Scott: *As I begin yet another day/a couple of words I must say/It shows that you care/and of your knowledge to others share/Thanks for the great work on my résumé!*

SQUARE PEG IN A ROUND HOLE

We dated for less than a month, until his lack of motivation began to get on my nerves; he couldn't hold even a temporary job for more than a week, let alone find full-time employment.

Me: *Can 48 hours already have gone by/without hearing Scott moan, groan or cry?/It's not that I'm worried, it's just that I care/and wonder if he's having much wear and tear/Besides, it's now Friday . . . you know what that means/You can come out here for dinner, if you like franks and beans/Now don't make a joke of my rhymes or my pun/just let me know if you're up for some fun/You know how to reach me; I trust you do still/even if only to say if you won't or you will.*

Scott: *It's Friday, the weekend is here/Time for frolic and maybe a beer/It's time to go out, maybe dance/and, hopefully, drop down your pants/Get ready to have fun, my dear.*

The fun didn't last very long. On the verge of a nervous breakdown, Scott piled his belongings into his car and went to live with his widowed mother in North Carolina. Until a few years ago, he would send me rhymes on Valentine's Day, so I guess he's alive and kicking somewhere.

For me, it was back to the drawing board to place another ad.

45

MORE DATES

I have no idea how many gay and bisexual men live in and around the nation's capital, but there always seemed to be a new pool of candidates either running or reading personal classifieds in Washington's *City Paper* and *The Blade*.

My next date was with a guy named Guy, who asked me to meet him at a parking lot where we chatted for half an hour in my car. Though pleasant and rather good-looking, he had a girlfriend . . . and I wasn't willing to share anymore.

Ever meet someone who looks just like you? It can be pretty scary, but that was the story between Roger and me—same height, build, eye color, and neatly-trimmed beards. We had lunch at a Chinese restaurant across the street from a client's office. While waiting our turn for the buffet, wouldn't you know it, one of the workers I knew came in to eat there and got right behind us in line? I caught him looking at us throughout the hour.

"Is that your brother?" he asked. "You two could be twins!"

It was just too close for comfort; Mr. Roger also lived in my neighborhood. About a month after our lunch, I ran into him at the neighborhood Shell station, where he had taken his car for a state inspection. Seated next to him on the passenger side was a woman, presumably his wife, yelling at two

212

kids arguing in the back seat. He never even mentioned them to me, the bastard!

Then there was Richard, a born-again Christian who, before coming out, worked at Campus Crusade for Christ and Christ for the Nations. Fascinated by how an avowed believer could confess to being gay and live faithfully as a homosexual, a dichotomy I still hadn't resolved, we talked for two hours on the telephone and made plans to meet at the Black Eyed Pea next afternoon for lunch.

"I've always known I'm gay," Richard calmly explained, "and I don't believe that God makes mistakes."

"But almost every church and most religions teach that it's wrong."

"What's wrong? To be born a homosexual, or to love someone of the same sex? We can't control one, and the second is a natural expression of the other."

"I thought the Bible says it's *un*natural."

"The apostle Paul supposedly did. But I believe his words are subject to scrutiny and interpretation."

"Then you don't interpret them the way others do? You don't believe homosexuality is a sin? Lying with another man isn't an abomination? So why didn't God create Steve instead of Eve? Maybe we can't change what we are at birth, but we can control our behavior, don't you think? Shouldn't we be sacrificial—as Christ was—and live celibately?"

I had too many questions, and Richard didn't have enough answers. He had faith, though, and believed that God loved him just as he is . . . homosexuality and all.

There wasn't any chemistry between us, but plenty of potential for friendship. Richard said he was putting together a "coming out" group for closeted Christians. Would I be interested in participating?

We exchanged phone numbers, and he promised to call before the group's first meeting.

I had put my Christian creed on hold while I sorted out the competing claims on my spirit, soul, and body. Nonetheless, I still read my Bible and, slowly but surely, was coming to grips with what I believed the Scriptures said—and *didn't*—about same-sex love and expression.

46

HUBRIS AND HUMILITY

One last message appeared in my newspaper voice mailbox.

"I'm a Washington lawyer, but hope you won't hold that against me," the caller cautiously joked. "My name is Stuart; friends call me Scooter. People tell me I'm cute, but you'll have to be the judge of that. Give me a call. Let's see if we fit and if there's a match."

Scooter was 32 years old, five feet nine, and had the clearest blue eyes I'd ever seen. Yes, indeed, he was cute! At first, he reminded me of Mark Harmon; later, I thought he looked more like David Duchovny from *The X-Files*.

We sat in the Amphora restaurant, relaxed in a booth, our arms draped along the table and legs lazily resting upon the facing vinyl banquettes. The day was hot and humid, so Scooter was wearing shorts and a tank top. He was in good shape; it was obvious he worked out.

"So, what do you think?" he smiled at me nervously.

"I think you're real cute and would like to see more of you."

"Want to come back to my house, now? It's pretty close. We can relax in the hot tub inside, where it's air-conditioned and comfortable."

"Absolutely."

Scooter had a super spread. On one level was the kitchen, dining room and den, a living room, and a half-bath. Outside was the deck; upstairs were four bedrooms. We descended to a finished basement complete with its own bathroom and spa. Tossing our clothes off, we splashed into the Jacuzzi.

"Let's go upstairs," he bid me after a few minutes.

"Lead the way."

We saw each other regularly over the next few months.

There were no commitments, promises, obligations, or expectations between us, but we enjoyed being together. Permitting each other time and space, he respected my needs for freedom and privacy, and I respected his.

I took for granted that, whatever we weren't, we were monogamous with each other.

Scooter assured me that was the case. Despite what later happened, I guess he wasn't lying.

We generally saw each other on alternate weekends, either Friday or Saturday night. He would come to my place for dinner and stay the night. Or the other way around. I was quite content with the way things between us were going, and had no idea how frustrated Scooter had become.

One Friday night of a weekend when it wasn't our turn to be together, I decided to go downtown and hang out at a club or two. I wasn't looking to meet anyone or fool around . . . I just needed to escape from my Manassas doldrums.

Reaching Dupont Circle, I suddenly was overcome with this eerie feeling, a sneaking suspicion that I would find Scooter there. And he was. Standing with another guy, he was laughing and swirling his drink when I went up the stairs to the Frat House and literally bumped into him.

Surprised but glad—I think—to see me, Scooter gasped, "Bruce! What are you doing here?"

"I could ask you the same question," I replied, as I pawed my way through the crowded floor to a room in the back. When he wasn't looking, I ran down the stairs and rushed back home.

Later, he tried to explain what had happened and why.

"I was starting to resent our closeted little world. It made me feel like being gay was only okay behind closed doors," he began. "I need to feel normal, to meet other people who aren't so uptight about being gay. Neither of us has any gay friends around whom we feel comfortable being ourselves.

"There are other complicating factors, too. You have a relatively large, extended family. That also got to me, mainly because I couldn't see you dropping the heterosexual persona in front of them.

"I don't want to go through life afraid of being gay. I need to know I'm not some sort of aberration. I am what I am and shouldn't be afraid or ashamed to admit it. Unfortunately, I was beginning to feel that way when we're together. I got the feeling that if you went to a gay bar, you'd have such a stereotypical mindset about homosexuality that you'd backtrack home to shield yourself from it all. And that's just what you did."

"You never asked me to go with you," I complained, not mentioning that I had been to those places before. But Scooter wasn't finished yet.

"I'm beginning to need and want to share this aspect of myself with some close friends. I don't mean it in the joking sense, like you've done, passing it off lightly, while attempting to maintain a machismo demeanor.

"Like I said, I can't separate myself from you and the gay issue. I can't be gay—or accept it, at any rate—until I deal with it all. There's a time and place for everything, but I need to have gay friends, not just sex pals, which, I think, is how you view the gay scene. I need to know there are other people out that there who lead normal lives but still don't deny their gay side.

"I have to find out who I am. I'm glad we became friends, Bruce, but I can't lead my life in your bedroom. I know it's a rough journey for both of us. Hopefully, happiness will find each of us at the end of the rainbow. Someone is out there for you. Finding one another might not be easy, but I have faith it will happen for both of us. In my own way, I do love you."

Whew! In one fell swoop, Scooter not only upset my equilibrium, he destroyed my equanimity. It was humiliating, but I deserved it.

My hubris had been supplanted by a healthy dose of humility.

47

SHADES OF SCOOTER

"To thine own self be true."

The doctor's voice again reverberated in my ear. That's exactly what I thought I'd done. I wasn't a parade person and preferred to keep my own counsel. When my parents asked, "Are you seeing anyone . . . any plans to marry again?" I joked with them: "Only if I can find the right husband."

Amanda knew a little about this part of my life, but Barbara never did. And Jonah? I certainly wasn't about to make an announcement to him.

What was I to do?

I'd think about it tomorrow . . . after all, tomorrow was another day!

Tomorrow brought the latest issue of *Washingtonian* magazine and several new ISO personal ads. I answered and met three. Little did I know that they would be my last little escapades.

In his jeans, Weejun penny loafers, and a blue, button-down shirt, Jim was the consummate collegian. That was quite appropriate, since he worked as reference librarian at Towson State College. We found each other in the biography aisle of Brentano's bookstore at a Gaithersburg mall, then drove to the Baltimore house he still shared with his ex-lover. We watched dirty movies in the living room until it was time for me to go and look homeward, angel.

BRUCE H. JOFFE

With a Columbia University law degree, Marty had taken a different direction and moved to Washington to be a producer for the ABC-affiliated station's news. He stood five feet, seven inches—in his lift shoes—and had a pleasant face but a blemished personality. We saw each other for about four weeks, until a New York City station beckoned with more money, visibility, and potential to climb the roller coaster to greater fame and fortune.

My final gentleman caller was Terrence; one of the most intellectual men I had encountered, he served as curator at a Fredericksburg museum. From the photo he had included with his letter, he looked very sexy. When we spoke on the telephone, I asked him how old the photo was and whether it still reflected a good likeness.

"It was taken at least five or six years ago. Frankly, I've put on a little weight and lost more of my hair. Does that bother you?" Terrence inquired.

On the spot, I paused before answering.

"To be quite honest, yes, it does."

"Why?"

"Women should be soft, men hard and hairy," I quipped. "There's got to be chemistry for me. I mean, if there isn't traction where the rubber meets the road, all I do is skid."

He chuckled and then hit me with a question for which I was totally unprepared.

"Have you ever been in love with another man?"

"Yes, I have. No I haven't. Not in the way you most likely mean," I stuttered. "I have a few friends whom I love like brothers. But I've never been swept up in a passionate, committed, long-term romance with someone of the same gender. Why do you ask?"

"If you've never been in love with another man, then you haven't had the opportunity to make love with a male. It's not the same as having sex. One of these days it will happen, if you allow it, and you'll understand the difference. I hope, for your sake, it soon comes to pass.

"When—and if—you do fall in love, please remember our conversation. I'd like to talk to you about it, again. You'll discover that superficial stuff like weight and a thick head of hair aren't all that appealing. It's the bond, the sense of fitting with a soul mate, that truly matters.

"You've got a lot to learn yet," he said before hanging up. "I would have liked to meet you, friend, but I cannot be your mentor."

Shades of Scooter!

Hadn't I heard a similar message before?

Get with the program; it's time to move on and begin a new chapter.

48

Epiphany

I'm told that the things I had done, the tattered alliances I had devoured and let ravish me, aren't atypical. Many homosexual men need a period of adjustment, a time to come to grips with their repressed sexuality.

I wouldn't call it my promiscuous stage; I'd rather think of that time as an indiscriminate and transcendental age when I did some homework, even though my grades still suffered.

Contemplating my experiences since I had separated and divorced Amanda, I realized that Scooter was right. No man is an island or solo practitioner. We each need another, and for more than the night.

It takes putting a stop to minimizing who—and what—we are to know what we really, truly want . . . to be ready to receive and appreciate the gift of love and to humbly accept God's grace.

I'd reached the conclusion that being "gay" means more than acting on attractions to the same sex.

49

KING EGO

Superimpose the beauty of Rob Lowe on the dark masculinity of John Stamos, mix in a bit off Charlie Sheen for some spice, and add a dash of a younger Donny Osmond to good measure.

All right, I'll admit it: I still was hung up on looks and found Russ extremely attractive. But, hey, give me a break; looks are usually the first thing you notice.

Russ had suddenly appeared at the branch where I banked. Employed as "utility" staff, he worked at times as a teller, "on the rail," or was sent off "to shop." Translated, the jargon means that he floated around with temporary assignments. Shuttled wherever he was needed or wanted, customer service was his job this week, while posing as a customer and checking out other branches to see how well they followed bank policies was his next.

Twice that same day I made trips to the bank: once to make a deposit, again to cash a check. But each time my turn in line came, I was motioned to another teller line for assistance. And I couldn't stop looking at that gorgeous man with the beautiful face and dark, shiny hair.

Why didn't he turn and return my stare?

Russ was sent elsewhere to work for the next few weeks, and I had momentarily forgotten him. Then, one day, he reappeared.

I waited around until his shift ended, then followed him to the parking lot to see which car was his. It turned out to be a truck—a blue and gray Ford Ranger. Funny, it just didn't seem to be the image I'd envisioned for him.

As he opened the door, I wondered what my next move should be.

Lamely, I circled around in my car until his license plate came into view. KING EGO, it niftily read, and gave me an opening.

"That's quite a tag," I commented, letting down my window. "It sure outdoes mine, PR BIZ."

Not knowing what else to say, he laughed and said there was a story behind it. ("A good-looking guy driving a BMW in a Manassas parking lot? He must be lost and needs directions," was what he actually was thinking, Russ told me later.)

The next day, I pulled behind the bank to see if his truck was there. It was. So I parked, taking a pen and sheet of paper out from my briefcase. "If you're interested in having dinner with someone equally egotistical, give me a call," I wrote, along with my name and number. I added, "The guy in the gray BMW," since he wouldn't know who I was just by my name.

Inserting the note carefully under his left windshield wiper, I glanced around to make sure nobody was looking and then sped away.

My God, what had I done?

Never before had I been so aggressive, and I chastised myself for being that reckless. Not knowing what possessed me to take such a risk, I rushed back to the bank to remove the letter I'd left. His truck already was gone when I got there.

"Nothing ventured, nothing gained," I thought to myself. "What's done is done."

I would just have to wait and see what, if anything, would happen next.

* * *

SQUARE PEG IN A ROUND HOLE

Nothing occurred on Thursday. Friday was the night of my support group meeting. Rick, the guy organizing a group for closeted Christians, had finally put one together, and we were gathering for our second session.

Equally divided between men and women, there were about twelve of us, all told, sitting uncomfortably in Rick's Arlington townhouse. Most weren't Christians and hadn't come to discuss the Lord's role in their lives; what they wanted to talk about was their fear and coming-out experiences.

Taking turns introducing ourselves and explaining why we'd come, we passed around the pretzels, popcorn, and chips.

Heading back to Manassas around midnight, I took I-395 to the I-495 Beltway. As was my habit, I punched in my home number on the car phone to see if anyone had called. "You have two messages," the mechanical voice informed me.

One call was from Barbara, already reminding me to pick up Jonah the following weekend on Saturday before noon. The other came from him.

"This is Russ, alias King Ego," he hesitated. "I got your note and would be happy to come for dinner a week from Sunday, if that's all right. Give me a call. I live in Centerville and will be up for a while." Then he left his number.

Three times, I rewound and played back his message . . . trying to find hidden meaning or implied nuances imbedded in the three sentences totaling 35 words and a number. My heart racing a mile a minute, I was all thumbs and incapable of dialing. I would just have to return his call when I got home.

The thirty-minute drive seemed longer, like getting stuck in rush hour. Pulling my car into the garage, I ran upstairs to replay Russ's message. Prepared with pencil and paper, this time I transcribed each jot and tittle. It was too late, I suspected, to call him that evening. I'd have to wait until tomorrow which, after all, was more than another day—it was the weekend. Not knowing where he'd be or what he'd be doing on Saturday, I didn't want to call too late or too early. It was eleven o'clock the next morning when I finally picked up the phone to dial. And, wouldn't you know it, I got his machine.

225

"Hi, this is Russ. I'm not here now, so please leave a message. I'll return your call soon."

"Russ, it's Bruce. Thanks for your message. Sunday, the 26, is fine for me. I'll be in all day. Give me a holler, and we'll make more definite arrangements."

I never left the house, not even once, that entire day.

The phone rang several times, but it was either MCI or credit card solicitors calling to sell me their services. Just as I was slapping together a peanut butter and jelly sandwich for dinner, the phone rang again. It was now six o'clock and, at last, I recognized Russ's voice on the other end. Saying he was required to work two Saturdays every month, he apologized for getting back to me so late.

"No problem," I fibbed. "I've been in and out all day."

We talked about inconsequential stuff. Taking a week off from work, he was going to visit his brother on the Outer Banks, he said. It would be another week before he could come over for dinner.

I gave him directions and told him to be here around six.

50

NOT ON THE FIRST DATE

I can't remember the last time I had felt quite so dizzy and beside myself, with knots in my stomach, a low-grade infection hovering around my heart, and jitters all over. This was a giddy, slightly off center feeling, a muted but palpable sensation quite different from the explosive reactions I had had before with certain men. It was different, too, from the feelings of care and concern—and of love, I suppose—that I had experienced with Barbara and Amanda. Reaching back into the recesses of my memory while thinking about Russ and waiting for him to arrive, I realized the way I was feeling now came closer to those early hints of affection that had touched me many years earlier with Mary Margaret Ritucci, my first girlfriend.

Shaking my head, I surveyed the setting.

The table was arranged and everything ready, so I sat down to wait. In between cracking the kitchen blinds to peer out the window, I must have made at least a dozen nervous trips to the bathroom. Confirming that every hair was in place, clothes without wrinkle, I wanted to be certain I looked my very best.

At five minutes to six, I heard a door close and peered out the window into the parking lot. It was him. Russ parked in an unnumbered spot near my house and got out of his truck, holding a large bouquet of flowers. He tested the vehicle's doors to make sure they were locked, looked at the house numbers, then walked up to mine and lightly knocked.

I waited about thirty seconds and shouted, "Just a minute, I'll be right there," before going downstairs and opening the front door. Patience is a virtue, even when waiting a minute more hurts.

There he stood, more beautiful than I recalled or dared to imagine.

Removing his long topcoat, he was dressed all in black—but, on him, it was absolutely sexy. The tailored slacks were a fine fit; he wore a silk shirt with billowing sleeves, its two top buttons open. Shiny black shoes complemented the look, charmed by a tiny diamond earring delicately glimmering from the lobe of his left ear.

What a catch! Why was he working in a bank, I wondered, when he could easily have gotten a well-paying job as a model?

I led him upstairs to the living room, pointed to my collection of CDs, then told him to put on some music and make himself comfortable. Dinner was almost ready. In the meantime, I would be back in a second with some hors d'oeuvres and a bottle of wine.

We had a leisurely meal, talking about his vacation and our jobs. I got up to clear the table and stack the dishes in the sink.

"Let me help you," he offered, carrying over some plates and turning the water on to rinse them.

"Don't be silly," I responded, still playing the cordial host. "I'll do them later. Just leave them here on the counter."

"It's probably a stupid habit, but I always rinse my plates off before putting them in the dishwasher," he indicated. "I'd feel better about helping you, please, if you don't mind."

God bless him, here was a man after my heart!

* * *

We retired to the living room where a cozy fire awaited. Wineglasses refilled, we sat down next to each other on the sectional sofa. It was time to play twenty questions.

"So where did you go to school?" I asked.

"I went to a few colleges before graduating from George Mason."

"That's where I teach."

"Which department?" he asked.

"Communication. And yours? What did you major in?"

"First business, then psychology."

"When did you graduate?"

"Two years ago last June."

He looked slightly older than most of my students, but not by much.

"Do you mind if I ask how old you are?"

"Twenty-nine. You?"

I was fourteen years older than him. "Thirty-six," I lied, subtracting seven years from my age. Then quickly changing the subject, I pressed on: "Where are you from?"

"Near Virginia Beach, where people don't end their sentences in prepositions," he said with a straight face, before his little grin broke into a wider smile. "I'm sorry . . . forgive me, I couldn't help myself. It's just that you fed me one of my favorite lines from *Designing Women.*"

"Where are you from, *bitch?*" we cackled in unison.

Our conversation had become lighter and easier. I found out the TV shows, records, and movies he enjoyed, and learned that he went to the same church as I did, although he usually attended a later service.

"What do you do in your spare time? Where do you go to hang out?" I asked.

"Mostly Tracks, although I don't go into the city much."

Bingo! I'd hit the jackpot. It no longer mattered how many questions I had used up, because he had just given me all the answers I needed. It was all or nothing, now or never . . . time to get on with it and cut to the quick.

"Russ, would you be offended if I said something pretty personal?"

He looked directly at me and replied: "No, please, go ahead."

"I find you incredibly attractive. Would you let me kiss you?"

"I think you're quite sexy, too, and, yes, I would like you to kiss me."

Moving from my side of the couch to his, I put the palm of one hand on the back of his head and the other on his cheek. He came closer.

"Do you want to go upstairs?" I prodded him.

"Not on the first date," he apologized.

"Okay, then, don't move . . . I'll be right back."

I went upstairs and brought down a blanket, which I tossed over us as we got more comfortable by stretching out on the floor in front of the sofa.

For someone so *bonito,* he had an amazingly masculine body!

We lay together touching and holding, hugging and kissing, squeezing and stroking, for what felt like hours. And although we technically didn't have sex, it was the closest I had ever come to making love with a man.

To this day we joke about that, our first encounter. "I wouldn't go upstairs on the first date," Russ tells our friends. "But I was willing to take all my clothes off and get it on with him in the living room."

Sometime around two in the morning, Russ said he had to leave. Tomorrow was Monday and he needed to get up early for work.

"You're going to have to come back soon, you know," I warned him. "Now that we've had our first date, I want to go upstairs and spend the night together."

"I think that can be arranged," he said as he put his clothing back on, neatly folded and handed me the blanket, then left to drive home.

Alone in the bedroom, my body still tingled.

* * *

I waited two days before calling him again. He sounded genuinely delighted to hear from me.

"I've been thinking about you," he confessed.

"Tell me about it! So, when can we get together again? This time I won't accept any excuses. We're going to spend the entire night in my bed."

He just laughed.

"How does Thursday sound to you, the day after tomorrow? I'm working late on Friday and don't begin work until after noon."

We didn't eat any dinner that night.

* * *

Snuggling and spooning into each other, we found an ideal fit.

He must have been feeling the same way, because he quickly began spending more nights at my place than he did at his.

Sometime after our first month together, Russ asked what I would think about him moving in. He had been renting a room from college friends, a married couple who were expecting their first baby within a few weeks.

"They're going to want more privacy," he said. "Besides, I'd rather help with your mortgage payments than spend more money on rent."

I was delighted, to say the least. We rented a U-Haul, dismantled his four-poster bed, removed the bureau and night-stand, then carried cartons and boxes onto the truck filling up in the driveway.

"What do you have stashed in all of these crates?" I grunted, heaving a ton of cardboard containers aboard the moving van.

"Kitchen stuff: two sets of dishes and silverware, a bread maker, microwave, toaster oven, and several Cuisinarts of different shapes and sizes. They're packed in these cartons. Over there," he pointed to several even bigger boxes, "are my arts and crafts supplies: clay, bows and ribbons, dried flowers, and wreathes. In the cartons up front are Christmas ornaments and decorations for the tree: lights, window candles, and other seasonal fixings."

We spent the next week unpacking, making room for his things and putting them away. Unlike Amanda's piles and messes, Russ's belongings were all neatly stacked, organized, and labeled. Everything fit snugly somewhere, with nothing getting in the way.

Accommodating each other, room by room, we began building a nest.

51

PERFECT PARTNERS

In our partnership and plurality, Russ and I treaded on little common ground. I'm a garrulous Yankee; he's the soft-spoken Southern gentleman. I'm a morning person; he fares much better in the evenings. He's the chief cook; I do the dishes. He loves to garden and play in the dirt; I hate the bugs and prefer working out at the gym in air-conditioned comfort. I'm now his lifeguard; he's become my caretaker.

I love him for his kindness and gentleness, and for the endless ways he responds to my needs and desires; for his patience when I'm being ugly or difficult; and for everything he does daily to make me feel loved.

And, wonder of wonders, the feeling is mutual.

With handwritten notes on hundreds of greeting cards, we've shared our good fortune with Hallmark investments.

Naturally, not everything between us has been a bed of roses. There weren't any real thorns, just a few minor thistles.

* * *

Russ's mother called right after he moved in and planted a seed that could have sprouted some pretty ugly weeds.

"What can you possibly have in common with someone that much older?" she asked in her soprano voice. At sixty, Doris still resembled a young Elizabeth Taylor or Joan Collins, especially in her annual Olan Mills glamour shot portrait.

Neither Russ nor I particularly look our age, but there would always be those fourteen years between us. When I turned 50, he'd be just 36 . . . at 60, he'd be a youthful 46. I worried: Will he still need me, will he still feed me, when I'm 64?

"I've always had this picture of being married and growing old together—a little old man with his little old wife," I explained.

"That's nice," he argued. "But you wouldn't believe how many little old men come into the bank together, making deposits or withdrawals from their joint accounts."

My age and the lie I had originally told about it was resolved when I asked Russ to open an account for me at his bank. He did, and added a little something more of his own.

That evening, this poem had been deposited on my pillow.

Opening your account, one thing caught my eye:
Your DOB field did surprise!
I know that March 10th is the day you began,
but not '56 . . . '49!
Thirty-six or forty-three
makes no difference to me.
Whether eight or fourteen
years are between
our ages, I love you truly.

From then on, we would tease about the age difference—Jonah and Russ would add up their ages and remind me that the sum amounted to less than my years, but it didn't amount to any big deal. Nor is the age factor a problem anymore between his parents and me.

During a brunch at his aunt and uncle's house one Christmas, Russ's cousin complained about having to drive to Reagan Airport to pick up his fiancée during the holiday frenzy there.

"You could take the Metro, meet her at the airport, and then take the Metro back to your car," Russ innocently proposed.

"Russell!" demanded Doris. "What a horrible thing to suggest. No wonder you're still single!"

You could hear the rain drops outside as everyone around the table silently acknowledged the unmentionable. Russ took his mother aside later and let her know how much she had hurt him—and me.

"I'm *not* single," he said, taking my hand. "And I'm very happy."

"Well, I can't say that we didn't suspect as much," she admitted.

After many visits back and forth, they see that their son genuinely is happy. That's what they want most for him, regardless of who's the reason.

We all enjoy each other's company now, getting together for the holidays and a couple of times during the year in between. I believe they've come to accept and like me, and—in their way—love me, too. But it must be hard on them: two sons, both gay, no prospects of grandchildren.

* * *

To celebrate our first anniversary, Russ presented me with a gold wedding band. On Valentine's Day, two weeks later, I reciprocated.

For our second anniversary, we added a West Highland white terrier puppy to our little family, the two of us and my miniature schnauzer. On our third, a devilish little Scottie joined the fray. All three of our dogs were always well-behaved; we had no problems housebreaking or training them.

But we had outgrown our coop and purchased a two-story colonial, a real fixer-upper, which we moved into on New Year's Day in 1995.

I then learned something new about Russ: he's a very handy dandy.

Replacing ugly, old light fixtures, he installed new track lighting and dimmer switches; rewired or rerouted the electricity; and fixed our sump pump plumbing. He uses a level to hang rods and curtains, so there's never any doubt that they're even. He follows the blueprints, literally, and has no problem putting furniture together, despite those mislabeled, easy-to-follow assembly instructions.

If only relationships could come with such simple directions!

52

COMMITMENTS

How does one commit an emotion as intractable as love to a series of words on plain pieces of paper?

I'll never forget the first time total strangers noticed the closeness between us.

Russ and I had taken a vacation in Cancún and met Karen and Allison on the flight down. We guessed they were lesbians, but they weren't. They assumed we were lovers, and how right they were.

"How long have you two been together?" Karen inquired over afternoon margaritas. With her sexy looks and tousled, shag haircut, she could have worked as a stand-in for Michelle Pfeiffer.

"What makes you think we're together?" I asked her incredulously.

"I'm sorry," she apologized. "I didn't mean to offend you. It's just obvious by the way you two look at each other. Anyone can tell that you're in love."

Karen and Allison weren't the only ones who recognized the symptoms. After our return from Mexico, Angela Fletcher also commented on my good spirits.

* * *

"You've been in a remarkably upbeat mood for longer than I can remember," my business partner exclaimed after we left a meeting at the Greater Washington Society of Association Executives headquarters in Dupont Circle one afternoon. "Care to fill me in on the cause? What's going on?"

"Why don't we have dinner downtown and I'll fill you in," I proposed. "It's getting pretty late and doesn't make sense to get stuck in Washington rush hour traffic."

"Good idea," she agreed as we walked down the street. "Anywhere special you want to eat around here?"

"Nope. Just pick a place."

Angela meandered a few blocks before pushing open the door to a storied tavern. It took a few moments for her eyes to filter through the smoke and dim light. You should have seen her face when it dawned on her where she had led us: Mr. P's, a well-known gay club, was beginning to fill with happy hour patrons.

"Let's get out of here, please," she urged. "Why didn't you tell me what kind of place this is?"

"What makes you think that I knew?"

We walked another block before agreeing to eat at the Omni Hotel restaurant. We went down the few steps and waited to be seated. "No smoking section," she insisted, and gave the waitress our order. Over drinks, she plowed ahead.

"Let's hear it. What gives?"

"I'm in love."

"So, what else is new? Please don't tell me you're getting married again! I've exhausted my supply of wedding cards. Who is it this time? Do I know her?"

Not knowing how she would react, I cautiously broached the subject.

"It's not a her."

"I don't understand. You'd better explain."

"It's a him."

Angela regarded me silently for a few moments.

"Have I met this person?" she asked.

"Not yet, but I want you to . . . if you're willing."

"Why wouldn't I be willing?"

"Some people wouldn't approve. Do you?"

"Well, it really isn't my business, Bruce. But you know me. I'm pretty liberal and open-minded. I'm more concerned about you."

"Me? Why?"

"Because you're the one who's so image-conscious and concerned about what other people think. Does anyone else know about this? Have you told your family and Jonah? What about Barbara and Amanda? Do the people at work know? How are the gossip-mongers reacting to this juicy piece of news?"

"Slow down a bit, please. Apart from Russ's brother and family, nobody yet knows. Certainly not my father, Jonah, Barbara, or Amanda. Most of them know that Russ and I live together. I suppose they think we're roommates and very close . . . friends.

"Are you planning to tell them the truth?"

"That all depends on how things work out."

"What about Russ's brother? What did he say when you told him?"

"Nothing much. He's gay and always assumed his brother is, too. We went to visit Mike and Len at their place on the Outer Banks. Russ simply told them we wanted to sleep in the same bedroom."

"Who is Russ's brother? Mike or Len?"

"Mike. Len is his lover, although they prefer the term 'spouse.' They've been together about five years."

"You're going to have to give me some time to digest all of this," Angela warned. "You've hit me unexpectedly from left field. I have no problem accepting that you're involved with another man, if that's what you want.

But what does it mean? Are you now gay? Is he? Where did you two meet? How long has this been going on?"

I shared as much of our story as I thought she should know.

Angela wasn't a particularly demonstrative person, but she encircled me with her arms as we stood up to leave.

"I'm in your corner, kid," she promised. "Whatever makes you happy makes me happy, too. So when do I get to meet him?"

"Soon," I said. "After I break the news to a few other people."

* * *

Ralph and Suzanne, two friends from the health club, accepted my admission quite calmly. It was no big deal, they said. Anyway, both already knew about me and were glad I'd finally found someone with whom I was so compatible. Ralph had recently remarried. Ironically, his new wife was totally upfront about having lived with another woman in a lesbian relationship for five years before meeting him.

And my two ex-wives? Amanda stopped by to settle some unfinished business after Russ came to live with me. Her bloodhound instincts sensed something amiss almost immediately.

"Is he queer?" she fished.

"He's just as straight as I am," I answered, with only the slightest hint of sarcasm and a bit of indignation.

For her part, Barbara always considered the possibility, though she wouldn't admit or articulate it. "Why did I need to take in a tenant? What difference is there between a roommate and a renter?" I'm sure she wondered. Her friend Faith finally explained the distinction to her in a way she could understand. "Open your eyes," she insisted. "Why do you think Jonah refers to your ex-husband's 'friend' as his Uncle Russ?"

Jonah was fourteen-years-old then and knew much more than I did at his age. Kids today are relatively sharp, and most people expected that he had a pretty good idea about what was going on between Russ and me. What he really knew about our relationship and what he may have guessed, however, were two separate issues. I finally got up enough courage to address him and explain the circumstantial evidence he had surmised.

"What do you know about love, Jonah?" I opened our conversation.

He squirmed, a natural response from adolescents to that question when they fear it's a prelude from their parents to the birds-and-the-bees conversation.

"You know that Mom and I both love you?"

"Uh-huh."

"And that even though we're no longer married, your mother and I still love each other in a very special way?"

"I suppose."

"Do you love me?"

"Dad, that's a dumb question."

"Not really, Jonah, because love usually means accepting other people, even if we don't understand or agree with everything they do or feel. Do you have any idea what I'm talking about?"

"Not really."

An adult conversation with a young teenager can often be a monologue, with the parent doing most of the talking.

"What do you think about Russ?" I asked.

"He's okay."

"Do you like him? I hope you know how much he likes you."

"I guess so. It's pretty cool that he likes gardening and takes time to show me how and where to plant stuff. Did you tell him that I want to become a botanist?"

"Yes, I did. Because of his father, he knows a lot about flowers and plants and says he's happy to help you however he can."

"Why?"

"Because you're so important to me. And anyone who's important to me is very special to him, too."

"How come?"

"Because he cares about me, and I care for him. Does that totally shock you?"

"No, I knew you guys like each other a lot and spend all your time together. Don't you go out with women, anymore, Dad?"

"No, Jonah, I don't."

"Why not?"

"Remember when Amanda and I were married, how hard it was for all of us to live together and how hurt you were, feeling left out? I'm sure you haven't forgotten that, even if you don't remember the problems your mom and I had when the two of us were married."

"Yeah, Mom can be difficult."

"Difficult isn't the word! I don't want to say anything bad about your mother, but things don't always work out between husbands and wives—for a whole lot of reasons. Sometimes, however, you find someone who's easy to live with and, more than anything, really wants to make you happy. That can be very important and makes a big difference. Do you understand what I'm trying to tell you?"

"I guess so. You get along much better with Russ than you did with Mom and Amanda."

"That's right. And because we get along so well, we've come to share some special feelings. You're still a little too young to understand, but you will very soon."

"Are you saying that you and Russ love each other?"

"Yes, Jonah, I am."

"Does that mean that you're gay, Dad?"

With that little word, he'd nearly knocked the wind out of my sails.

"Words can sometimes be misleading, putting things into convenient categories that aren't always so clear. Does that make sense to you?"

"I guess so."

"Let me put it to you this way, Jonah. Because Russ and I love each other and live together like we do, yes, many people would call us gay. But others have quite a different idea about what the term means. They think gay people can't fall in love or enjoy a real relationship. They treat gay people and probably most other minorities as second-class citizens, not wanting us to have any rights, respect, or even religion. People like that think all gay people jump around from one bed to another. I want you to know that's not true. Many men, and women, have loving relationships and are committed to each other, much the same way as married people. Am I making myself clear?"

"Yeah. Can we talk about something else now?"

Funny, my father reacted much the same way when I told him the facts of life about Russ and me.

"You're old enough to make your own decisions," Dad told me. "I accepted your brother's lifestyle and didn't object too loudly when you decided to become a Christian. You know what you're doing, I trust. Just make sure you're careful."

So much for my *laisser-faire* dad. My mother—may she rest in peace—was probably turning over in her grave.

* * *

Yes, people know about us. And do you want to know something? I no longer care what they think or waste my time worrying about it.

Our friends already know the score, whether they've asked us or just assume. Neighbors are aware, too, about the two guys who live together on their street. Since we moved in, though, their property values have soared, and they smile when they see us.

We're making efforts to come out, too. Russ joined a club for gay gardeners and I belong to a group of "sexual minorities" in marketing and public relations. We've also become pretty involved in our area's gay and lesbian community.

One major issue, though, remained to be resolved: reconciling our religious beliefs and sexual orientation.

Damned if you don't, damned if you do.

53

RELIGIOUS RENEGADE

"But you're going to burn in hell, Bruce. Is that what you want, or don't you even care anymore?"

Rosie Greene and I hadn't spent much time together since Amanda called her before our divorce, disparaging my Christian character and behavior. Although we hadn't been in touch much over the last year or two, I assumed Rosie and I would always be friends. I valued our relationship and generally respected what she said. That's why I accepted when she asked to meet me for lunch. We sat in a restaurant having this talk.

"God has plans for you, Bruce. Don't throw them away and become a religious renegade. You have so much to give, it hurts me to say what I feel I must."

She opened her bag and pulled out a worn Bible from which she extracted a list written on a legal size pad of yellow paper. She tore off a sheet and handed me the paper. Listed in a hurried handwriting were several Bible references, each cited completely by book, chapter, and verse.

I looked down the roster, which I'd seen in other contexts before, and began by laughing, "Rosie, not even one of these clobber verses is included on God's all-time Top Ten."

"Be serious, please," she implored.

Seriously, I have difficulty with the way some people interpret the words they attribute to God. I'm especially leery of would-be evangelists who use the Bible to suit their own purposes. Maybe I'm sensitive because of my Jewish background and because of Christians who've damned us with faint praise. More likely, it's their misguided interpretation of Scripture that has caused so much hatred and persecution of the original chosen people.

"After all," claim these zealots, "don't God's own words condemn the Jews?" They then point out numerous Bible verses to support their hateful convictions.

I give credence to the Bible as God's revelation, but I believe the New Testament—the Old, as well—was written by men who misunderstood each other, fought amongst themselves, and spoke in emotionally charged terms like so many Christians do today. Human they were. Inerrant? Highly unlikely.

Since I've come to know Christ, I have experienced a variety of understandings and interpretations of what would seem to be irrefutable doctrine. I've been disappointed by the hypocrisy I've seen and the falling out between some of Christianity's most revered leaders from all denominations, persuasions, and self-serving bully pulpits.

I've come to believe we all are sinners who fall short of divine expectations. The fault lies not in our faith or beliefs, but in our human vulnerabilities; hence, we cannot base our Christianity on other people's expectations, but on God's amazing grace.

In the eyes of many church leaders, an individual who continues to live as a gay while claiming to be a Christian is more than mistaken—he's in a state of demonic deception. Homosexuals cannot be pleasing to God without denying their inherent sexual orientation, their propaganda trumpets. As far as I am concerned, they're out of tune with what God says.

Christ didn't die for the saints. He was crucified for us sinners.

Must I now somehow earn God's love through my actions and deeds? Need I sacrifice an intrinsic part of my self to be acceptable to God? I used to think so. What's the point, then, to God's gift of grace? There's no compelling reason to accept New Covenant promises if you're still going to be judged and condemned by Old Testament standards.

* * *

"Rosie," I said, returning to our conversation, "I believe that some of these verses are open to interpretation. Others are overly simplistic and must be understood within a specific context. I honestly think the church has injected questionable meanings to these passages, preaching adherence to traditions falsely portrayed as precepts of nature, the laws of God. And they're not. Some of them no longer are applicable; others empirically have been proven false; and yet others need to be taken with a good grain of salt."

"It's not a cafeteria, Bruce. You can't pick and choose what you're willing to swallow."

When I first became friends with Tom and Rosie Greene, they were committed Catholics but not born-again believers. Recently, however, their convictions had become much more fundamentally charged.

"Touché! So let's talk about these verses. Where should we begin?"

"How about starting with Paul?" she proposed.

"Fine with me," I granted, stipulating some ground rules, like, before wagging a finger at someone else's beliefs, you'd better take a good look to see how many fingers are pointing back.

"Tell me, was Paul free from all judgmental error?" I asked.

"Many of his writings deal with situations which occurred in other locations over two thousand years ago. His judgments come against a background of moral decadence where people experimented, willy-nilly, with every sort of sexual depravity, including pederasty. Could it be that, like most people back then, Paul considered everyone to be created heterosexual? Maybe when he says that homosexual behavior runs against nature, he's really talking about a heterosexual person who—against his basic inclinations—engages in homosexual activity?

"Paul's letters don't deal with loving relations between two persons who share the same sexual orientation, so they shouldn't implicitly be read as condemning all such behavior," I proposed.

"Don't you believe there's a critical difference in passing moral judgment on straight persons indulging in 'gay' sexual behavior and true homosexuals expressing their love? Biblical tradition knew little if anything about homosexuality per se. The few times it was mentioned, the writings were solely concerned with the commission of homosexual acts.

"Homosexuality isn't just some kind of conduct. It's a lifelong condition for which people aren't to blame," I maintained.

The New Testament's strongest argument against homosexual activity comes from Romans 1:26, where such acts have been translated into English as being "against nature."

But, what did this phrase really mean for the apostle, who also said, *Does not the very nature of things teach you that if a man has long hair, it is a disgrace to him?*

Every picture I've seen of Jesus depicts him with long hair—and I dare anyone to tell me that he was disgraceful!

54

Proof-Text Theology

"Are all homosexual acts manifestations of sexual perversion?" I asked Rosie.

"Must we accept that what most Bible translations refer to as homosexuality truly represents the mind of biblical authors about this sexual orientation as we know it today? The pervert isn't a genuine homosexual, but rather a heterosexual who engages in homosexual practices . . . or, maybe, a homosexual who deceives others by sleeping with the opposite sex.

"Personally, I think Paul was talking about pagans who go beyond their normal inclinations, indulging themselves in a smorgasbord of sexual deviations. Such acts are voluntary choices to act contrary to their ordinary sexual nature, orientation, and identity."

Lumping homosexuals with the wicked who wouldn't inherit God's Kingdom, Rosie had more of Paul's statements—specifically I Corinthians 6:9-10 and I Timothy 1:9-10—listed. My reaction to them was pretty much the same.

"Take a closer look," I suggested. "Every text in the Bible that deals with acts of homosexuality also mentions aggravating circumstances: idolatry, prostitution, promiscuity, rape, seduction of children, and inhospitality."

"By inhospitality, you're referring to Sodom and Gomorrah?" she quickly jumped in.

"That's right. Throughout the Bible—both Old and New Testaments—the sin of Sodom was never understood as homosexuality, but rather as selfishness, pride, neglect of the poor, and inhospitality to strangers that culminated in rape. The men of Gibeah in Judges 19 weren't homosexual rapists; they were sexual degenerates."

I sounded as though I was delivering a sermon.

"All these texts you point out are primarily concerned with something other than homosexual activity, itself. Boil them down to three major issues: abuse or exploitation of others, ritual purity, and betrayal of Jewish identity.

"It may shock you to know," I whispered conspiratorially, "that some people believe—apart from rape, child molestation, or intentionally hurting a loved one—it's difficult for two consenting adults to commit a serious sin in a sexual gesture."

"Then how do you explain what it says in Leviticus?" she countered.

Gotcha! Rosie had pounced on the only place in the Bible where God apparently does condemn homosexual acts between men:

> *Do not lie with a man as one lies with a woman; that is detestable . . .*
> *If a man lies with a man as one lies with a woman, both of them have done what is detestable. They must be put to death; their blood will be on their own heads.*

"That book was written when Israel's role was to serve as a nation of priests . . . when ritual purity, the holy superiority of men, and the virtue of procreation separated Jews from the heathen," I submitted.

"I've been taught that Christ did away with all such restrictions when he fulfilled the law and added grace: *Do not call anything impure that God has made clean.* Read it yourself, it's in Acts 10. Need additional confirmation? Check out Ephesians 2:14-15.

"You're the one who warned me about not picking and choosing Scriptures out of sync with today. So explain this one to me," I argued. "The Old Testament says, *No one who has had his testicles crushed or his penis cut off shall marry into the Lord's community.* Where does that leave all those good heterosexual men who've chosen to undergo vasectomies? Come on, Rosie, we can't be so selective in our interpretation of Scripture!"

* * *

Paul preached on the superiority of marriage and subordination of women. Women, he says, should dress modestly, with decency and propriety, not with braided hair or gold or pearls or expensive clothes. If he could only see how gussied up in their Sunday best women get for church! And how many accept his assertion today without any reservation that, *if there's anything women want to know, let them ask their husbands at home* . . . let alone that women aren't qualified for ordination to the priesthood?

Granted, the Catholics do, and I guess I respect their all-or-nothing approach, even though I do disagree with much of their dogma. Still, how does the Vatican explain its good sisters serving as educators, when even the apostle Paul says he doesn't permit women to teach or have real authority?

Paul says he *wants men everywhere to lift up holy hands in prayer without anger or disputing.* Try doing that in most churches and see how quickly you'll be given the right foot of fellowship.

And how many pastors can honestly admit that they manage their own families well and see that their children obey them with proper respect? After all, asks the apostle Paul, *If anyone does not know how to manage his own family, how can he take care of God's church?*

What Paul wrote to the Pharisees of his time, I believe applies, just as well, to today's Philistines: *. . . if you rely on the law and brag about your relationship to God; if you know his will and approve of what is superior because you are instructed by the law; if you are convinced that you are a guide for the blind, a light for those who are in the dark, an instructor of the foolish, a teacher of infants, because you have in the law the embodiment of knowledge and truth—you, then, who teach others, do you not teach yourself? You who preach against stealing, do you steal? You who say that people should not commit adultery, do you commit adultery? You who abhor idols, do you rob temples? You who brag about the law, do you dishonor God by breaking the law?*

No, I'm convinced my understanding of many biblical edicts and injunctions is more reasonable than what I've heard proclaimed by the "religious right"; but absolute conviction is something much more tenuous.

"The depth of our human misery," wrote one of the authors I had read, "is that we are never completely certain whether we are obeying or disobeying God." How true! I wish I could remember who said that.

* * *

"You'd be amazed at the number of scholarly books on the subject, as well as the multitude of committed Christians who, apart from this particular 'blemish,' are active in the church and evangelically-oriented," I told Rosie.

"My question to them has always been the same: How can you reconcile your beliefs with such an obvious departure from conventional Christian teaching? How can you love another person of the same sex and profess to be a believer, following Jesus?

"While their answers differed depending upon individual experiences and backgrounds, one point was almost universally made: Our God is a god of grace who loves us unconditionally.

"To tell homosexuals that, to enter God's Kingdom, they must cease being homosexual—or at least stop expressing their sexuality—is to put them under the law rather than grace. Homosexuals cannot earn salvation by sacrificing their sexuality any more than heterosexuals can!" I insisted.

"We can't choose our sexual orientation; it's a given, dare I say a gift? To pray for a change is about as realistic as praying for my eyes to change colors from green to blue. Believe me, I've tried. Internalizing self-hatred isn't healthy, nor have I been called to a celibate life.

"Yes, some people claim that there are victims who've been changed from a homosexual to heterosexual orientation through Christian conversion, prayer, exorcism, Spirit baptism, or divine healing. Nonetheless, I've found that truly 'reversed' people are rare, and there's little valid evidence that they even exist. Research shows that most are truly miserable; sooner or later, they always return to their innate identities."

* * *

I could tell that my diatribe was disturbing Rosie. Drumming her fingers on the table and nibbling on her lower lip, she rolled her eyes up in exasperation. But I couldn't stop. Not yet. Not before flushing out the torrent of torment that had been building up inside me and now finally had burst.

"Does homosexuality represent a deviation from God's divine order?

"Does God intend all human beings to be heterosexual?

"Does God make mistakes—so many of them?

"Is God so sadistic that maybe one-tenth of all the people he creates—millions and millions of them!—are gay, with no choice in the matter and no hope of changing . . . and then God denies them, under the threat of eternal damnation, the right to express their sexuality in a loving relationship? Certainly, I pray not.

BRUCE H. JOFFE

"A brochure on the door of the Episcopal chaplain's office at Stanford University asks, 'What did Jesus say about homosexuality?' Open the brochure and its pages are completely blank. Jesus himself said nothing regarding homosexuality in the four gospels, but spoke more about the sins of the spirit than the sins of the body. Isn't it possible, Rosie, that Jesus would have condemned the Church's oppression of lesbians and gays?

"Show me where any scripture clearly condemns sexual acts between two men or women who love each other. Wasn't David's love for Jonathan said to be wonderful, *passing the love of women?* Could Ruth and Naomi have been lovers? Were Daniel and Nebuchadnezzar's chief eunuch? Is it so blasphemous to believe that Jesus had a special love for another man, John, his beloved disciple? And why, when enlightening his disciples about the second coming in Luke 17:34, did he state: *I tell you, in that night there shall be two men in one bed; the one shall be taken, and the other shall be left?* Why two men, Rosie? Jesus could just as easily have said 'a man and a woman in one bed' . . . or 'two men fishing' . . . or two men doing anything else but being in bed? Why this example, then?

"Few heterosexual couples even merit a mention in the New Testament, so the fact that little is said about same-sex relationships isn't unusual. But I believe that one such relationship *did* make it into the Gospels. In his encounter with what may have been a homosexual man, Jesus offered no harsh words of condemnation. Instead, he went to extraordinary lengths to heal the man's sick companion. I'm referring to the Roman centurion in Matthew 8:5-13, who begs the itinerant rabbi to heal his beloved servant.

"Sure, Matthew could have included this story simply to illustrate that Jesus had a heart for outsiders. But the Greek text and linguistics can be understood to suggest an intimate physical and emotional relationship between this Roman of rank and his special 'servant.' I can't help but wonder: Did Jesus extend his compassion to someone even further beyond the bounds of acceptability than the reviled Roman centurion . . . but, more specifically, to a Roman centurion who engaged in sexual relations with another man?

"Here, as elsewhere, I suspect that homosexuality remains an open question. The sheer possibility of same-sex relationships in the lives of important biblical characters suggests to me that the Bible may be more accepting of homosexual love than most people would imagine."

* * *

I was on a roll now, and couldn't stop myself from lecturing. But Rosie rapped her knuckles on the table, then grabbed my wrist and demanded attention.

She had come prepared with more of Paul's verses, these from II Timothy 4:3-4: *For the time will come when men will not put up with sound doctrine. Instead, to suit their own desires, they will gather around them a great number of teachers to say what their itching ears want to hear. They will turn their ears away from truth and turn aside to myths.*

"We're not here to have a heated discussion on theological hermeneutics," she granted. "I don't want you to lose your salvation; that's all that really concerns me. I fear you're sinking into a hellhole which is going to swallow you, to destroy your eternal life if not your life here and now," she seemed to sob.

"Tell me: what do you think God expects from you?" she inquired.

"You want to know what I think the Bible *really* preaches?" I asked. "Have reverence for God; respect one another; be loving and kind, forgiving and merciful, honest and just. And just as important, be tolerant of others. We all need to learn how to tolerate our differences and not be so damn judgmental. God calls us to unity in love for him and each other, not mere uniformity in our traits.

"To be acceptable to God, must we conform to all the church's teachings, see ourselves as intrinsically disordered, and believe our desire for sexual expression is a tendency toward evil? Are we to repress sexual feelings? Is that what it's all about, Rosie?

"Our concept of sin isn't the same as God's. We tend to prioritize sins in a hierarchy of lesser to major. I don't think that God looks at sin like that. All sin—no matter how minor or major—is repugnant to him. And while nobody knows for certain whether God blesses loving relationships between two people of the same gender, I do confess my sexual behavior along with all my shortcomings . . . those which I'm aware of and those of which I'm not . . . in my prayers.

"Scripture reveals a Christ who welcomes those the world shuns and despises, those who are aware of their guilt.

"Again, I ask you: Don't you find it interesting that Jesus himself says nothing against homosexuality? What do you think he was referring to when he said, in Matthew 19:12, *There are eunuchs who were born that way from their mother's womb* . . .

"Frankly, I can't find a more accurate description of the homosexual condition as we now understand it!

"Jesus implies, I believe, that 'eunuch' applies to all people who are sexually different. The prophet Isaiah predicted that, after the Messiah comes, eunuchs would be accepted as full members of God's new community. Isaiah's prophecy came true in Acts 8:26, when the Holy Spirit led Phillip to baptize the eunuch who was reading Isaiah and intent on understanding what his message means.

"What does it mean? I'll tell you what I think: That God's house is to be a place of prayer, of worship, and of welcome, for *all* people."

55

GRACE UNDER FIRE

I caught my breath and took a sip from the soda glass still sitting full before me. The bubbles were gone now; it was flat and without fizz. What more could I say? How could I mitigate the anguish my words had caused this dear friend whose heart was in the right place, even if her holier-than-thou attitude offended me?

"I guess what I'm trying to say, Rosie, is that my Christianity is not a function of compliance with all the laws, warnings, and edicts in Scripture. If it were, I'd probably be content to have remained a Jew. But my faith, belief, and hope of salvation are found in what I believe to be the New Covenant's cardinal principle:

> *For it is by grace you have been saved, through faith—and this not from yourselves, it is a gift of God—not by works, so that no one can boast.*

"This concept of grace . . . of God's love . . . is the cornerstone of my hope for forgiveness and ultimate redemption.

"You ask me how I can claim to be a believer when my life doesn't reflect that belief? You say I cannot be a Christian because my lifestyle seems to contradict biblical principles. And you charge that I'm leading astray all who may listen to what I have to say with an open mind and heart.

"I, however, beg to differ. To recall a silly saying, we shouldn't reject the message for the messenger! Returning to my basic conviction—God's grace, mercy, and forgiveness—and where we started this conversation, remember what Paul said? *But by the grace of God I am what I am.*

"Contrary to what you or others may think, I did not choose to be what I am. It's not a matter of feelings or human emotions; it's something more basic, essential, and genetic. Over the years, I submitted myself to marathon prayers, fasting, penance, Christian self-help groups . . . you name it. But I believe that Gestapo tactics can never really change who we are.

"Whether I am sinking into a hole that only gets darker and deeper, which may destroy my very physical life and will steal away my eternal life, I have no definitive answer. What I do have is hope—and faith—based on the grace I believe is the New Covenant's underlying message.

Rosie reached out and placed her hand on top of mine. She had run out of words to argue and ammunition to fire. The look in her eyes as they met mine was more forgiving and hospitable now, as if she somehow sensed that we just might meet in heaven and share a last hurrah.

* * *

My God is a loving and merciful parent who doesn't punish his children for something about which they have little or no choice.

I refuse to believe the love that unites Russ and me in a committed and faithful relationship is sinful, that it separates us from God's love, or condemns us to eternal damnation.

There is therefore no condemnation for those who are in Christ Jesus . . . For what the Law could not do, weak as it was through the flesh, God did: sending his own Son in the likeness of sinful flesh and as an offering for sin.

SQUARE PEG IN A ROUND HOLE

Now, as always, the mystery of faith is that the Almighty Creator uses imperfect people and words to convey eternal truths.

The overall principles by which God wants his children to live never change. How they're interpreted and preached, however, depends on many factors.

From *in the beginning* to the last *amen,* there's no finality about the ideas presented in Scripture just because the pages in the book have come to their end. The God of my Bible lives and still has the last word.

Epilogue

Two artists' prints in our home illustrate the dichotomy of my life. The first is in the foyer and faces you, coming and going. Called "The Laughing Christ," it's a lithograph by a Jewish man named Fred Beyer. Russ ordered it for me one Christmas from a *Playboy* direct mail solicitation.

Relatively small, the portrait is a masterfully done pencil sketch in brown and black sepias. It depicts a Semitic Jesus who seems to be enjoying a good joke . . . or maybe he's having the last laugh?

Mouth opened wide in a joyous smile, there are creases on his face and lines under his eyes. Parted in the middle, long hair falls on both sides of a large brow and down onto his back. Head slightly tilted, his eyes—somewhat squinted—seem to regard you as they follow your movements. Over his heart, long, tapered fingers gently touch a few folds in the robe that he wears. He is not at all handsome, but imbued with vitality.

Love emanates from his presence. A man of humor, not sorrow, he reaches out to grip you with a life-affirming spirit. Because it captures his offbeat humanity, this is quite a different picture of Jesus than most.

The other print is much larger and adorns a bigger but less prominent wall. A Thomas Blackshear III serigraph entitled "Forgiven," it's rendered in shades of pastel water colors and shows a much more familiar savior.

BRUCE H. JOFFE

Here Jesus stands behind a young, good-looking construction worker. Holding a hammer, the worker's hand has just driven the nails that crucified Christ. Yet the fallen man is held, uplifted, and loved by a holy redeemer.

Blackshear's inspiration is found in Psalm 130: *If you, Lord, kept a record of sins, O Lord, who could stand? But with you there is forgiveness.*

* * *

More than two hundred years after the Declaration of Independence proclaimed that we all are created equal, the country's largest Protestant denomination finally admitted that slavery is sinful and asked forgiveness from African-Americans for the church's role in advocating segregation.

The message preached from many Southern Baptist pulpits had been that God ordained the separation of the races, and that tampering with the status quo would deliberately contradict the Almighty's inviolable will.

Posting a "godhatesfags.com" Web site, one Baptist leader made quite a scene picketing the funeral of a martyred gay college student killed in a senseless hate crime. In a national broadcast, Pat Robertson prophesied fire and brimstone falling on Orlando, Florida, because of the rainbow flags flying during Disney's annual "Gay Days." The Boy Scouts appealed an "activist" judge's decision that the organization couldn't discriminate against gays. And, before he died, the Rev. Jerry Falwell preached that the terrorist attacks on 9/11 were prompted, in part, by "the pagans, and the abortionists, and the feminists, and the gays and the lesbians . . ."

Over on Capitol Hill, the Employment Non-Discrimination Act didn't make it to the floor of the House or the Senate. After the House Majority Leader referred to a homosexual congressman as Barney "Fag," and another Republican went on record castrating "homos" in the military, did anyone really think the bill stood a hell of a chance?

SQUARE PEG IN A ROUND HOLE

Bill Clinton's people already decided there was no compelling reason for the federal government to become involved in a Supreme Court case that would determine whether states have the right to pass anti-gay legislation. Donning latex gloves before admitting them to the White House, our forty-second president's Secret Service insulted a group of visiting gay dignitaries.

A federal judge in Virginia upheld Clinton's "Don't Ask, Don't Tell" policy, ruling that the military can discharge people just for stating they're gay. The judge said the policy is "not based on prejudice," but that it serves a legitimate need: protecting the privacy of heterosexual service members.

Despite all its pomp and circumstance, the "W" Bush Administration conveniently forgot about removing from combat military men and women who decided to be honest and to come out during the invasion of Iraq. I guess they needed more corps and didn't care whether our loyal lesbian and gay soldiers returned home or were ultimately discharged in a box.

An Anglican rabble-rouser from Nigeria trespassed on sacred ground because he'd had enough, but wanted more. Objecting to the egalitarian Episcopal Church (USA) electing a gay bishop, confirming female leaders, and judiciously agreeing to bless same-sex unions, the African bishop was determined to discount American churches and steal their sheep.

Protecting the "sanctity of marriage" supposedly threatened by those of us in committed, same-sex unions, fools rushed in with vitriol and passed constitutional amendments in many states, allowing us even fewer freedoms.

If all of us are created equal, what has become of the "decent respect to the opinions of mankind" about which the Declaration so clearly speaks? Hasn't our Creator endowed us with certain inalienable rights—liberty and the pursuit of happiness, among them? I thought they were guaranteed to all U.S. citizens by our Constitution and its Bill of Rights.

Someone, please, explain why our families, religions, government, and culture make some folks feel so queer that they prefer hiding in a damn closet rather than come out and prove there's nothing but a bunch of smoke and mirrors behind all those emperor's new clothes.

Who, really, knows?

We each are part of a divine design in all its grand diversity.

Yet, for reasons unknown that now must escape us, like square pegs, we have trouble fitting securely—no matter how we try or twist and turn—into society's series of oblique round holes.

Mysterious creatures we are, it has been said. And that, after all has been expressed or excoriated, it truly doesn't matter.

No, from my point of view, I doubt that it matters much in the end.